It's Never Too Late to
Achieve a Dream

FINALLY
FIT

JOHN H. CLARK III

https://www.fossilfit.net/

DEDICATION

This book is dedicated to anyone and everyone who feels that life is passing them by; and that it is too late in the game to do anything about it.

It is not too late.

Scores of people have supported, encouraged, and inspired me during my journey from a depressed and hopeless, aging couch potato to a determined and eager go-getter who for the first time in a long time is genuinely excited about the future.

Hats off to the entire pole vault community, an incredible group of folks from all around the world who have touched my life in so many ways, and are too numerous to mention individually.

Having said that, I have to single out my fellow Houston native, Scarborough High School graduate, dear friend and brother, Bubba Sparks, who for some reason decided to take me under his inspirational wing, so to speak, and help me transform myself and rejuvenate my life.

I'm forever grateful.

And my loving wife, Katie, whose undying support through all my ups and downs over the past 20+ years makes everything possible. Without her in my corner, the story would undoubtedly be a lot different.

CONTENTS

FOREWORD

by Doug "Bubba" Sparks

In a parallel universe, since I left high school, my dear friend, John Clark, and I have been working our way towards connecting.

A few years younger than me, he was mainly friends with my brother and his circle of friends when we were kids. When we were both eight to 12 years old, we played Little League baseball and football at the same place – the Oaks Dads' Club in Houston, Texas. We both graduated from Scarborough High School, and then life happened.

Many years later, a random Facebook exchange brought our orbits closer together once again. Such is the world these days.

First, John made a friend request to me. We saw each other's posts, which led to a direct message. I had been preparing for the World Masters Games in Auckland, New Zealand, in the pole vault. The WMG is our Olympic Games, held every four years, with five-year age groups from 30-100+, typically with 30,000+ athletes from over 100 countries.

I went on to win the gold medal, which led to John's reaching out to me with a – to him – crazy question: "Do you think

I could take up pole vaulting for the first time in my life at 60 years old? I'm a couch potato, way out of shape, and I would like to maybe try it if you don't think it's crazy."

"Absolutely not! Let's go!" was my response.

And that was the beginning of a great friendship. For better than a year, John would meet me every Sunday near my house in Austin and we would drive the one hour each way to New Braunfels, where we would pole vault at my coach's place. We had conversations about anything and everything on the drive, and the vault part was an evolution for both of us. I found that John is an accomplished artist, has written a dozen books, plays guitar, and has hiked the 500-mile Camino trail across Spain – TWICE!

As an athlete, I found John to be a superb student, as you may expect from a career teacher. He was patient; he would stop before he got hurt; he was willing to take steps backwards, and even avoid progressing too fast, if he felt he hadn't mastered the previous steps. This is very non-vaulter behavior, and, in many cases, very non-male behavior.

His reward was 3rd place in the Texas Senior Games, and then he became the Oklahoma Senior Games champion, earning a gold medal – along with a great sense of accomplishment. My reward was the pride in watching this man change his life, and the addition of a great friendship.

Surprisingly, this is actually just the beginning of John's new life.

He got his personal training license so that he could help other older couch potatoes find his version of the Fountain of Youth. Who better to learn from than someone who was where you are just a little more than a year ago? He has begun volunteering at no less than three vault facilities. He went to the National Pole Vault Summit at Reno in January, vaulting a lifetime best in the process of meeting the greatest vaulters in the world.

Life's a journey and not a destination. John says he's a changed man and his future is full of optimism. I don't know the old John, but I love the John I got to know, and I'm so grateful to have been able to witness this part of his journey.

After 54 years of vaulting, how cool is it that I learned so much about life and vaulting from a total beginner? I'm also grateful that we will spend our final years as great friends.

Love you, brother.

I've got no idea what you will come up with next, but I know it will be fun!

———

Matt Stone, best-selling author, fitness enthusiast, and nutrition expert

> *"When someone exceptional does something exceptional, it's kind of nauseating. Are they just trying to rub salt in our wounds of mediocrity? But when someone ordinary does something extraordinary, it has the power to move mountains. That's John Clark and 'Finally Fit.' He's so typical of all of us that you'll be really compelled by his sudden and spontaneous jolt of inspiration to take on the seemingly impossible (learning how to pole vault at over 60 years of age?), and you'll find yourself daring to dream of what YOU might really be capable of, as well. He's got me thinking about starting rock climbing at 41, and believe me... I ain't got no climber's body to work with!*
>
> *"If you're feeling like life has passed by too quickly, or that you're no longer capable of what you once were, John Clark's story is just what you need to re-ignite the spark inside you."*

———————

Shawn Francis, elite pole vaulter, coach, mental health and athletics vlogger

> *"Bronnie Ware, an Australian nurse who cared for patients in the last 12 weeks of their life, wrote a book called, "The Top Five Regrets of the Dying." Intentional or not, John Clark filled this book full of tools to avoid experiencing those same regrets on your death bed.*
>
> *"He writes from a place of experience where he steps outside his comfort zone – from backpacking all over Europe, to picking up the pole vault at the age of 60! As someone who has danced with depression my entire life, the honesty and vulnerability John displays in telling his story is stunning. As a former elite pole vaulter, following John pick up the sport at 60 is a great reminder why I fell in love with the sport in the first place. Bronnie Ware wrote about the regrets of the dying, but John Clark's story makes you want to live!"*

INTRODUCTION

I was not ready for this to happen.

Not ready at all.

It's not like I hadn't had time to prepare. Not like I shouldn't have seen it coming and been at least somewhat geared up. This thing that hit me like a ton of multi-colored candle wax was not some sort of big surprise sprung on me at the last second. I should have been ready.

But I wasn't – not in the least.

So what was it? This big thing that happened?

My 60th birthday.

When I turned 60 years old, it was a nightmare.

Seriously.

The reality of being 60 years old, for me, was traumatic. Unsettling. Depressing. Devastating. All of those things.

How did this happen? *When* did this happen?

Am I really … 60?

WTF?

I remember when I was a kid, going to visit my Grandma and Paw Paw on the weekend at their place on Sam Rayburn Lake in east Texas. For a while, everybody camped out in a three-car garage on their little peninsula overlooking the lake, sharing space with a boat, rods and reels, tackle boxes, nets and bait cans, life jackets, inner tubes, gardening tools, lawn mowers – all kinds of necessary lake stuff. Then they built a nice, little house next to the garage. I don't remember how many bedrooms it had, but I remember having my own bed to sleep in, and Paw Paw waking me up to go fishing when it was still dark outside.

He had unique ways of rousting people out of bed – like flipping on the light and throwing a tray of ice cubes in the bed, or tossing the poodle on top of you.

"Hurry up – the fish are bitin'!"

Anyway … back then, my grandparents were probably in their 60s, and they were OLD people, man. Now I'm one of those old people, like them?

Good grief … really?

Not only that, along with now officially being old, my life kinda sucked. I was stuck in a difficult and highly stressful job that I mostly hated, spending a lot of time on the couch, staring at the TV and self-medicating to numb my distasteful reality, 40 pounds overweight, out of shape, suffering ongoing bouts of depression and anxiety, and just plain tired.

I was a bit of a mess.

Same old thing, day after day after day.

Life, I felt, was passing me by, and part of me did not care.

Part of me just wanted to hurry up and get it over with.

From the outside looking in, I'd had a fairly successful life at that point, by most standards – college degree; published author; successful careers as an engineering draftsman, and then a journalist before I became a junior high school English teacher; married; happy, healthy kids – but I also was carrying around an extra-large plateful of regrets, and felt like I had come up short in so many ways.

Made so many bad decisions; so many stupid mistakes. Wasted so much time; so many of my talents.

Now, I'm 60 years old? Ten more years, and … heavy sigh. I need another beer and a shot, please.

Then, one day I was sitting at home scrolling through Facebook on my phone, and I saw a post from a guy I knew back in my childhood days, named Bubba Sparks.

Bubba was several years older than me, so we were never actual friends back in the day. I don't think we ever even had a conversation. I was friends with his younger brother and sister, and our parents knew each other from the years the kids all played sports at Oaks Dads' Club in the Oak Forest area of northwest Houston, and we all graduated from the same high school.

Anyway, Bubba – who was a standout pole vaulter in high school and a three-time national champion in college – posted something about a world championship "Masters" track and field meet in New Zealand, where he took first place for his age division in pole vaulting. This was sometime around April 2017.

I sent Bubba a friend request, and he accepted it, and I read a bunch more stuff about him pole vaulting all over the world, winning championships, setting records. I messaged him about it – he remembered me, or pretended to – and he told me the story of how he quit vaulting sometime after the 1976 Olympics (he was an alternate on the U.S. team that year) and went into business, but then got back into vaulting years later after discovering the USA Track and Field's Masters program for older athletes.

That sounded pretty darn cool. I thought back to my days running hurdles and relays in junior high, and wondered if maybe I could join the old folks' track club.

Quitting sports when I was 15 years old has always been one of my biggest regrets – something I still look back on and wonder, what if? What if I had stuck with it? I was a good athlete and played sports year-round. Sports was my life – and my identity – for a long time, and when that went away, I spent more than a decade sort of wandering around, lost in a fog, pretty much stumbling through life.

What if?

I thought about the old guy running events I might be able to participate in, and then I thought, 'What about pole vault?' I remember seeing Bubba and the older guys over at the pole vault pit during track practice – our school was a combined junior-senior high – and I knew a kid from Oaks Dads' Club who pole vaulted in high school. Hmm …

Eventually, I sent Bubba a message: "Is it ridiculous to even think about learning to pole vault at my age (60 in August)? Be honest."

He answered: "Absolutely not. There's a guy our age out near Clear Lake (Texas) who used to vault. He would be a good start place for info. There's also a small group that jumps at The Woodlands High School on most Sundays. I've got many other connections who can help find a fit, but there is absolutely no reason to not start."

And the rest is history.

I started learning to pole vault. Got back in the gym and started working out again. Practiced vaulting every Sunday. Entered some senior track meets and actually got good enough to qualify for the National Senior Games.

It is a bit of an understatement to say that my life has turned around considerably.

I'm healthier and happier than I've been in at least a decade. For the first time in a long time, I'm excited – excited – about the future. I have big dreams again. I'm setting goals, and I'm taking action to achieve those dreams. Some things on my list already have been checked off. Completed. What's next?

Sure, I'm probably in the 4th quarter of my life now (football reference there), which means there are a lot more years behind me than in front of me. And, yes, I wasted a lot of that time that is now gone and never coming back. I made tremendous mistakes, bad decisions, and bone-head moves.

But it's OK now.

I've still got that 4th quarter, and I can still win the damn game.

Really, it's not how you start that is important – it's how you finish that counts.

For a long time, I was sitting on the bench, watching other people play, pretty much just waiting for the clock to run out.

Now, I'm back in – and I'm in it to win it.

And guess what?

You can do it, too.

Read my story and be inspired.

Anyone can re-start, jump-start, kick-start their life at any age, at any time, under any circumstances. It takes two things: making a decision; and doing the work.

Whatever you want or have ever wanted out of life – go for it.

It doesn't have to be anything to do with sports, athletics or physical fitness. Dust off that lifelong dream you gave up on and stashed way back in the hallway closet of your mind. Look at it. Hold it in your hands. Embrace it again.

What is the dream?

Learning to play a musical instrument?

Traveling overseas and riding the trains through Europe?

Opening a restaurant?

Moving to New York City?

Starting your own company?

Riding a bicycle cross-country?

Sailing across the ocean?

Earning a million dollars?

Running a 10K?

Becoming a movie star?

Writing a book?

Getting a college degree?

Remember how it felt to dream that dream?

Now, go for it.

Why not?

Depending on the source providing the information, average life expectancy in the U.S. is right around 76 years for men, and 81 years for women. Divide those numbers by four. Which quarter of the game are you in? How much time is left on the clock?

Guess what? This is the last game of the season, and when the fourth quarter ends, that's it.

Don't waste any more time. Give it all you've got. Don't give up. One play at a time. Leave everything on the field.

When are you going to start?

Why not today?

You're never too old, and it's never too late.

Here's what I did, and here's what I'm doing.

The story of my comeback.

Let's go.

———

"The only thing that stands between you and your dream is the will to try, and the belief that it is actually possible."
– Joel Brown

johnclarkbooks

CHAPTER

ONE

Standing on the runway at the University of New Mexico Track and Field and Soccer Complex in Albuquerque, a 12-foot pole vault pole in hand, ready to make my first jump at the 2019 National Senior Games, I felt fairly calm and relaxed.

About an hour earlier, when I arrived at the stadium and started getting ready to warm up, I was so nervous I put my knee brace on the wrong leg.

I did manage to get my shoes tied OK, but I could barely breathe. Maybe the 5,000-foot elevation above sea level had something to do with it, but my stomach was also tied in knots, and so I spent a fair amount of time taking deep breaths, trying to settle down, as I jogged up and down the track, stretched, did some vault drills, took some practice jumps.

Just go out there and have fun.

Enjoy the experience.

It was a long way from nearly two years before, when on an almost-summer afternoon in the middle of June, I'd probably have been sitting at home on the couch, watching TV, drinking beer or thinking about drinking beer. Fat and depressed, bored stiff, wondering what I could be doing instead, but deciding, nah, maybe I'll do it tomorrow.

Now, here I was, one of more than 13,000 senior athletes from all across the country gathered together for the largest event of its kind.

Me.

An athlete.

Competing on a national stage.

Wow.

As the pole vault officials worked to clear up some sort of confusion so we could get the competition started, I looked around at the huge stadium, where I later saw Flo Meiler of Vermont, the oldest female pole vaulter in the world at age 85, not only set a new world record, but keep jumping to improve that mark not once, not twice, but five more times.

I watched across the way as septuagenarians, octogenarians, nonagenarians, and centenarians ran and threw and jumped in front of cheering crowds.

The morning after my event, as I headed over to the pole vault pit to watch the women's competition, I noticed a commotion out on the track, so I stopped and saw a tiny, very slender woman standing in one of the middle lanes, outfitted in a colorful track uniform and racing bib, a meet official by her side. She was stepping back and forth, one foot in front of the other, bouncing up and down a little bit, staying loose. There was nobody else lining up for what appeared to be the start of a race, just her.

I asked someone how old she was, and they said, "Ninety-seven."

Finally, the starter appeared with blank pistol in hand, took his position, said, "Ready, set …" and boom!

Off she went, moving at a pace not unexpected for someone approaching 100 years old, but with as much focus and determination as any Olympic athlete.

I got a lump in my throat as I stood there and watched Alabama resident Mary Kemp run the 200 meters – halfway around that collegiate track – all by herself, in a record-setting time of 2.09.73.

Amazing.

A friend I met last year at the Oklahoma Senior Games, Don Isett, 80, set a new National Senior Games record when he vaulted 8-feet, 2 ½ inches, then narrowly missed another world record at 9-0 ½. Don set a world record 10-6 back when he was 75 years old.

I've met and befriended all kinds of incredible people since I started pole vaulting, and they have all welcomed me with open arms. It's the most extraordinary bunch of people.

After I got warmed up, caught my breath – and put my knee brace back where it belonged – I went and got in line on the runway to get in some practice jumps. As I walked up and stood behind the last guy, he turned, smiled, and extended his right hand, "Hi, I'm Gary."

It was Gary Hunter from Indiana, a former college all-American who has set world and national records in three different USATF Masters age divisions.

Just like that. No big deal.

"Hi, I'm Gary."

It's like that everywhere you go.

Finally, everything was set.

John Clark III was the first name on the starting list – seems like it was always that way back in school, too – and so there I was, pole in hand, crossbar sitting at what should be an easy 1.85 meters, a little over six feet.

When they called "bar set," and waved the white flag across the runway, it was show time. I didn't want to think about it too much, so I lifted my 12-foot Fiber Sport pole, rocked back once onto my right foot, left foot planted 41 feet from the pit, and took off.

Counting each time my left foot hit the runway – four, three – start dropping the pole tip into the metal box – two, boom, boom!

Lift-off.

Reach high and extend the arms. Jump and drive the right knee up, similar to a layup position in basketball, and swing hard with the left to bring the hips up and over the bar.

My friend, Don Curry, who was jumping later in the same group and eventually won our division, told me after I climbed out of the pit that I cleared the bar by "at least 18 inches."

It was soon my turn again, and this time the bar was raised to 2.00 meters, a little more than 6-6. Since I was so far over the first time, I didn't change anything – my run distance or grip height – and cleared easily again.

Next bar, 2.15 (7-0 ½).

Again, easy clearance with room to spare.

I had no idea at the time that the bar was going up in six-inch increments. The posted progression was: 1.85, 2.00, 2.15, 2.30 (7-6 ½), 2.45 (8-0 ½), 2.6 (8-6), 2.75 (9-0), 2.9 (9-6), and so on, but I didn't know enough to check such a thing – and I'm glad I didn't.

Each time the announcement came that they were raising the bar, I knew it was my turn again, and I went over, found my mark, and jumped.

At 2.30, easy clearance.

Then 2.45, over easily.

When I walked off the landing mat after that one, my friend, Cyndy, who was using my camera to take pictures, came walking up with a big smile on her face and said, "That a new P.R.?"

I had no idea.

I really didn't think so. I thought the bar was still sitting somewhere around 7-6. After checking with the women charting the official results, sure enough, I'd just cleared 8-0 ½ for the first time ever, a new personal record.

So many times since I nearly cleared 8-1 at the January 2019 National Pole Vault Summit in Reno, I'd tried to get that height, but my head always got in the way. Not literally – I wasn't knocking the bar off with my noggin – but psyching myself out. Thinking too much. Trying too hard.

Believe it or not, there are many comparisons between pole vaulting and the game of golf, and trying too hard in either of those two things is pretty much guaranteed to produce less than desirable results.

In both golf and pole vaulting, you have to concentrate on the process, and not worry so much about the outcome – the results. Take a good stance, proper grip on the club, make a good, smooth swing, and chances are high that you'll hit a good shot, and the ball will go where you want it to go. If you get out of your rhythm, try to force the ball – steer it – toward the target, the outcome will likely not be good.

Same thing in vaulting.

You have to focus on making a smooth, accelerating run, strong plant, aggressive take-off, big extension, swing the legs and keep the hands moving. Do those things correctly, and the outcome will take care of itself.

Absolutely true, but a lot easier said than done.

So, when I heard them say the bar was now going up to 8-6, everything changed. My brain told me I had to jump higher. So far, I'd been clearing bars easily, without giving it much thought. I had moved my grip up a couple of times, and moved my run back 10 feet (two steps), but now I decided to move back another two steps, to 61 feet, and raised my grip some more.

Don asked me if I was comfortable running from 12 steps. I told him I was – and I *thought* I was – but in all three attempts at 8-6, I never ran with as much rhythm and confidence as I had been up to that point. I tightened up, started trying to force things, instead of being smooth and relaxed, and I missed on all three attempts.

Damn.

The thing about it was – it was all in my head. I could have made that height.

But I was happy.

Really happy.

I was fairly confident going in that I'd jump at least 8-feet and set a new P.R., because I'd worked fairly hard over the past five months or so, and I was hoping to possibly finish in the top 15 for my age group.

Turns out I finished at no. 8.

What an incredible culmination of a highly improbable journey that began nearly two years before when I saw that Facebook post from Bubba.

———————

CHAPTER
TWO

One of the best life lessons I ever learned was in a Journalism 101 class in college.

I'm pretty sure that was not the official name of the course, but it was a beginning newspaper reporting class, taught by a female professor whose face I can still picture very clearly, but whose name has probably escaped my memory forever.

A lot of water has gone under the bridge since then, but I think it was the first day of class, and this professor walks in, introduces herself, says a few things about this and that, then immediately gives us our first assignment:

Get up, she says, take a pen and a notepad, go out across campus, and interview three people about registration. Come back and write a story.

Registering for college classes in those days was a tedious, time-consuming ordeal. There was no on-line registration back then. You went to some administration building and stood forever in long, long lines and signed up for the courses you wanted. It was bad enough at the University of Houston, where I went. I can't imagine what it was like at some monstrous place like the University of Texas, which includes the population of a good-size small town.

So, registration was definitely not any fun. Not something anyone ever looked forward to – and that was the assignment.

Go out and get comments from three random people on campus, then come back to the classroom and write a news story about student reactions to registration.

When the lady professor finished talking, she stood there, arms crossed, looking at the class, smiling. The silence in the room was deafening. There were probably two dozen young kids in the class – and me, the elder statesman at age 27. I had never worked at a school newspaper or any other kind of newspaper, but I was majoring in journalism with plans to become a sports reporter. I didn't know about the rest of the students, but there was a lot of hesitation, people sort of looking sideways at each other, apparently not quite sure what to do next.

"Go ahead," the professor said. "I'll see you when you get back."

I couldn't hear anyone's thoughts, but I suspect the consensus might have been something like, "What? Is she kidding? Go out and interview three people? On the first day?"

And this is where that lesson that I've never forgotten comes in.

I was sitting there like everybody else, butterflies now churning, a little confused, intimidated, nervous, scared.

But I had a decision to make.

Do you want to do this or not? Do you want to be a reporter? If you do, then you don't have any choice.

Get up and go do it.

So that's what I did.

I picked up my notebook and my pen, walked out of that classroom, went and found someone walking around who looked approachable, told them who I was and what I was doing, asked them about their experiences with registration, and took notes. Then I did it two more times.

And I lived through it.

Now, I don't remember much of anything else about actually doing those interviews, and I don't remember what kind of story I wrote. But I'm pretty sure that was not the point of the exercise. That was not the lesson to be learned that day.

The lesson to be learned that day was – do you really want to do this?

You do?

Then, get up and go do it.

And that lesson has come back to me a number of times in the years since.

———————

CHAPTER
THREE

When the day dawned on that milestone 60th birthday of mine, I was in a pretty desperate state.

Some days, honestly, I just didn't want to live anymore. I was really, really tired. Tired of getting up early in the morning, groggy, dreading the day, slogging through another miserable eight or nine hours at work, getting wasted at night, going to bed early, waking up and doing the same thing all over again.

My maternal grandfather committed suicide about 30 years ago, and I thought about the same thing from time to time, but I've always heard it described as a permanent solution to a temporary problem, and I believe that. I also always thought about that being my ultimate legacy, and I didn't want that to be the end of my life story.

I didn't want to be remembered for that – especially by my kids.

To me, and this is strictly my opinion (I understand there are many sides to the issue), a person who feels they have no other options, particularly someone who is old and infirmed and suffering, should have the right to choose their own death. I've always thought what Paw Paw did – although incredibly sad and I wish he were still around – was pretty damn brave. All his life, he was strong and active and independent, only to become almost completely incapable of caring for himself and probably on the way to a nursing home, which was something he always said he would never let happen.

So he took matters into his own hands.

If I am ever in the same situation, I wonder if I'd have the same courage.

Nevertheless, while killing myself maybe sounded like a good idea sometimes – sweet relief – it wasn't really an option. I actually loved life, and as far as I know, this is the only train ride we get to take. I just wanted to stop being so unhappy. You know, maybe stop the world and let me get off for a while. I'll be back later.

Unfortunately, I just didn't see any way out of the quagmire I was in. I was stuck in so deep a rut that I couldn't see the top of it, much less climb my way out.

How did I wind up like this? How did things get so screwed up?

It all seemed so hopeless. The ship was sinking, and I didn't know how to stop it.

Like I said, my list of accomplishments at that point seems fairly impressive, I suppose. Not a bad life at all – on paper.

For me, though, nothing is ever really good enough. For people with the "sickness" of perfectionism and insecurity that I have had all my life, no matter how high you climb, it's never high enough.

Accomplishing a goal feels good for a little while, but that satisfaction soon begins to go away, and the search for that same good – but temporary – feeling continues.

Sounds a lot like mind-altering substances. That first little euphoric buzz that you get from your substance of choice may feel really good, but it fades, and that's what you keep chasing over and over again with more sips, more shots, more hits.

You're after that same, first good feeling, but the cruel trick is, you never find it.

———

I grew up in Houston, Texas, in a blue-collar family with a younger sister and brother. We lived in a small, three-bedroom, one-bath house on a corner lot in a neighborhood alongside families with names like Pangarakis, Kasse, Baranowski, Furlow, Campbell.

There were plumbers, firefighters, mechanics. Kenneth's dad wore a tie to work, but I don't know what he did for a living. Chevys and Fords in the driveways. Kids up and down the block playing baseball, football, hide-and-seek, riding skateboards, bicycles, roller skates. Parents sitting outside in lawn chairs, visiting and watching.

One time a bunch of us were playing baseball in the next-door neighbor's front yard when they weren't home. I was at bat, and I lined a pitch that would have been a foul ball down the first-base side – except this was a small front yard, and so the ball crashed straight through their living room window.

All the kids – including me – took off running.

Then the words, "Johnny, we saw you!" stopped me in my tracks.

Across the street, my mama's friend, Mary, and her husband, Jimmy, were sitting on their front porch, watching the game. I had no choice but to trudge the rest of the way back home, and tell my dad I broke the window. Surprisingly, there were no major repercussions that I remember. Maybe he thought I was being honest – only because I had to – and so he went and bought some glass and fixed the window. No yelling, lecturing, or spanking involved.

My dad was a big guy who enjoyed working with his hands, and he was good at it. He repaired printing presses for a living back in those days, and he loved to work on cars. He rarely smiled, didn't talk much, and was not a touchy-feely, lovey-dovey kind of person.

The whole time I was growing up, he never once hugged me, told me he loved me or that he was proud of me. Not because he didn't or he wasn't, but because he didn't know how. Such a thing just never occurred to him – because that's how he grew up. In his world, it just wasn't done.

His dad was a stern, non-smiling, provider-for-the-family; a carpenter and stonemason, who was never home much. My father was the baby of the family, with four older sisters, and the three oldest girls apparently suffered, shall we say, severe disciplinary measures that might be considered against the law these days, whenever the old man was around.

When my dad was a little boy, my grandfather apparently took after him with a limb from a discarded Christmas tree, drew blood from switching him across his bare legs, and as the story goes, realized the error of his abusive ways at that point.

The amazing thing to me about the relationship between my dad and his dad is that they never once said, "I love you," to each other. My granddaddy never said it to his son, and his son never said it to him.

Even when the old man lay dying of cancer in a hospital bed in downtown Houston, neither man knew how or thought to say, "I love you."

So that's how I grew up.

I always wanted my dad's approval, but never did enough to earn it – in my young mind, anyway.

All As and a B on the report card. Good job, son? Nope. Instead of that, what I got was, "What about this B?"

Next report card, solid As, all across the board. Great job, son? Way to go? Nope. What I heard was, "You could've done that the last time."

Classic stuff.

The result of growing up that way was that my "self-worth tank" was never filled. I've always been an approval-seeker, and dependent on the opinions of other people to determine my opinion of myself.

I never understood that everyone who has ever been born has the same inherent value, just because they're a human being. No one is better than anyone else. We are all the same inside. Everyone is important, and good, and worthy, no matter what they do or don't accomplish. No matter what kind of grades they make in school, how many home runs they hit, or how many games they win, what they do for a living, how much money they make, what kind of car they drive, or how big a house they live in.

Like the old adage about how, no matter what, we all wind up in the same size hole in the ground, six-feet deep.

In my mind, everything was tied to accomplishments. For a long time after I graduated high school, the first thing I asked somebody when I met them was what they did for work. Then, depending on their job, I placed them in a certain category, ranking either above or below me in some kind of societal pecking order, if that makes any sense.

I either felt a little superior to them, because I had a "better" job, or I felt inferior to them because they had a better job than mine.

A really screwed-up way of looking at things, and that's how I went through my entire life – basing my opinion of myself on other people.

Kids I grew up and went to school with were millionaires. Doctors, lawyers, business owners. Lived in huge houses and drove fine cars. Some were retired and traveled the world. Never mind the fact that others were homeless, drug addicts, career criminals who had been in prison several times, or just everyday working stiffs like the rest of us.

In my mind, I was somewhere in the middle of all that, and obviously had fallen way short of the mark.

———

CHAPTER
FOUR

As the year went on following my 60th trip around the sun, something shocking occurred that finally got my attention a little bit.

I noticed one day that my hair was falling out.

Seriously!

There was a small spot in front, near the part, and another back at the crown, where my hair was considerably thinner than everywhere else. I couldn't believe it. Losing my hair was something I never even considered. Every time I got a haircut, no matter where I went, the stylist almost always said something about me having "a lot" of hair, nice and thick. That was one thing I thought I'd never have to worry about.

Now, all of a sudden, it's starting to fall out? That can't happen. As insecure and self-conscious as I am – I still have a hard time looking at myself in the mirror – I can't go bald. I just can't. My head is shaped like an egg on its side. I'll look ridiculous. This cannot be happening.

I've always been a believer in alternative medicine, holistic-type things. Since I was diagnosed with depression and anxiety 15 or so years ago, I've tried all kinds of treatments: hypnosis, acupuncture, Reiki, yoga, counseling, supplements, meditation, medication.

For about a year, I had been using essential oils for stress and sleep, and in my research for that, I had also read about them being used to treat hair thinning and hair loss.

I knew someone who had an essential oils business, so I messaged her about it, and she invited me to come over, so I went and we talked about various mixtures to use, and I ordered some products and started oiling up my head at night with concoctions of lavender, rosemary, cedar wood, thyme, peppermint, clary sage.

My friend also suggested a holistic "doctor" she had been to in a nearby town, who had helped her with some sort of ailment that I can't remember anymore. The idea was that something inside my body was going haywire and causing my hair to fall out. It made sense to me, because I knew I was completely stressed out all the time, depressed, not sleeping right, and drinking too much alcohol. My system had to be taking a beating.

Supposedly, this doctor would be able to examine me, diagnose the issue or issues, and prescribe a regimen of supplements that would help restore my system to proper working order. I was desperate, searching for answers – a dermatologist told me nothing could be done about my hair – and so I called the next day to make an appointment.

This holistic doctor was a young lady, probably in her mid-30s, very attractive, charming, and charismatic. As I told her my situation, she sat across from me, up on the examination table, and proceeded to tell me about her own background with a lot of the same issues as mine. She then had me trade places with her up on the table, gave me a poking and prodding examination designed to detect weaknesses in my various internal organs, and outlined a program of natural supplements.

This went on for a few months, and who knows if there was any effect from it, but something extremely important eventually happened.

During one of my follow-up appointments, we had talked about my experiences in the past with counseling, and this young lady mentioned a counselor friend of hers who she said was terrific, and maybe I should consider trying some psychotherapy again.

I've never given much credence to therapy, although I'd never done it for any significant length of time. Never really gave it a chance. It seemed like they always want to go back and review your life step-by-step from the moment of birth, and you just keep going back and back and back for session after session, it goes on and on and on, and nothing ever really happens.

So I thought about it for a while, and finally decided to give it a shot.

It was probably one of the best decisions I've ever made.

———————

CHAPTER
FIVE

There was a several-years stretch there, after I got back from my first visit in 2011 to the historic Camino de Santiago pilgrimage in northern Spain, when I was fairly happy and doing OK.

I was in the midst of sort of a midlife crisis then, and doing something fairly spectacular like taking my first trip overseas and hiking hundreds of miles across a foreign country by myself was terrifying in the beginning, but pretty satisfying in the end, and gave me a nice sense of accomplishment and satisfaction.

Finally, I felt like I had done something big.

Not long after that trip, through a series of fortunate events, I got a side gig as a proofreader for a small book publishing company called Archangel Ink, and that led to the start of my career as an author.

I had already written and self-published my first book, which at that time was titled "Finding God in Texas." I'd always wanted to write a book, and at that time I was having a lot of questions about God and spirituality and blah, blah, blah.

As a kid, our family went to church on Sundays and Wednesdays, but for me, it was mostly socializing, hanging out and playing basketball with my friends, going to dances, sneaking away from services and walking down to the corner store to buy candy, stuff like that. About the only lasting impact those seven or so years had on me was creating a profound fear of this invisible thing called God, that was going to send me straight to hell one day if I ever did *anything* wrong.

By the time I turned 15, and figured out that I could actually say "no" to my father and get away with it, I started refusing to go to church, and aside from a brief stretch in my early 30s, I never went back until I was around 45. My wife had started going to a small church near where we lived, and she eventually got me to start going with her by convincing me to try playing guitar in the praise team band, which performed religious songs during services.

I did that, and even let myself be appointed to the board of trustees, but after about three years, I'd had enough. Church just isn't for me. I have my reasons.

But anyway ... so I was having lot of questions about heaven and hell, the Bible, this and that, and I knew from experience that if I had questions about something, then other people (at least some) probably had similar questions. So I decided to use my journalism background and travel all across the state of Texas, and interview random people about what they believed in and why.

After the first couple of interviews, it became apparent that this book was going to be a lot more than just a collection of different people's viewpoints on God and religion. The stories people told me about *why* they believed whatever they believed were fascinating, to say the least, and produced an excellent little book that I self-published under what I thought was a clever title, "Finding God in Texas." When it first appeared on Amazon, I was thrilled. It even sold a few copies – mostly to family and friends.

After I got the proofreading gig, I mentioned to the company co-owners that I had written a book and would they be interested in taking a look at it. They said, sure, and so I sent them a copy of the manuscript, and they liked it enough that they wanted to revamp it a little, give it a new cover, different title, and re-issue it under the Archangel Ink imprint.

So "Finding God in Texas" was reincarnated as "Finding God: An Exploration of Spiritual Diversity in America's Heartland," and it remains one of my best sellers. My next book published by Archangel Ink was about my trip to Spain – "Camino: Laughter and Tears Along Spain's 500-mile Camino de Santiago." And things went on from there.

My writing and publishing rampage went on for several years, and I was doing other things like playing guitar in a little rock-and-roll band, but like everything else, the shine of these new endeavors eventually began to wear off and by 2015, I was slipping back into the abyss.

I went back to Spain two more times after that first trip, took a solo trip to Costa Rica, and spent two weeks driving the famous Route 66 from downtown Chicago to Santa Monica, Calif. Back home, I was still writing books, and freelancing every week for a local newspaper, but that good ol' depression was rearing its ugly head once again.

By 2017, I was a bit of a mess.

———

Flashing back to my teenage years – no pun intended – when I first discovered the wonders of altering my consciousness with various legal and illegal substances, I spent most of my spare time in a fog, of one kind or another.

After I quit playing sports in high school, I was lost. My identity was suddenly gone.

Beginning when I was eight years old, I played sports. That's what I did, and that's who I was. If I had a good game, I felt great. I was worthwhile; had value. If not, then I was inferior; worthless; a loser. Performance was the way I measured my worth as a human being. It was the only measuring stick I had.

For me, sports was everything.

When that went away, I was a ship completely without sails. For the next year or so, I was kind of in limbo, so to speak.

Back in my day, high school kids were divided into various cliques, including: the jocks (athletes), the freaks (long-hairs who smoked weed), the shit-kickers (cowboys), and the Jesus freaks (wore little wooden crosses around their neck and carried a Bible around).

All through junior high and into high school, I was a jock. Those were my friends, and that's mostly who I hung out with. After I quit athletics, I had no group. I didn't belong anywhere – until a kid who moved into my neighborhood, just down the street from me, introduced me to marijuana.

This kid had an older brother who smoked pot, and one day he said that he'd found a large stash in his brother's bedroom closet. Labor Day weekend was coming up, and his parents were going out of town, he said. He could pinch some of his brother's weed, and I could come over and spend the night, and we could get high.

I knew plenty of people who smoked pot – like the freaks at school, who always seemed to be having a helluva good time, and had really hot girlfriends – but for me, it was something taboo and scary.

Fascinating but frightening, at the same time.

Back when I was still going to church and sneaking away from service to walk down to the corner store and buy Hot Tamales candy, two of the kids I hung out with tried to talk me into smoking pot while we were out.

"During church?" I said.

"It's the perfect time," one guy said, smiling.

No way in hell I was going to do that. Be all stoned riding home in the car with my parents? They'd be able to tell, for sure. Not a chance.

But for some reason, this seemed like a good opportunity, so I took it.

When I stepped across that line, I thought it was the greatest thing. Not just the feeling of being stoned, but the side benefit that came from smoking weed was that it gave me instant access to the freaks club.

At last, I had an identity again. I wasn't floating around in outer space anymore, searching and reaching for something to hang onto.

I belonged somewhere.

This was my junior year, and I started growing my hair longer, smoking pot and cigarettes. Got a job and a car, hung out with the freaks. Made a fool of myself a few times getting wasted because it really wasn't me. I was pretending to be somebody I wasn't meant to be.

My senior year of high school, I basically missed out on, because I was hardly ever there. I only needed two credits to graduate, so I took two classes first thing in the morning, left school at 10 o'clock every day and went to work.

Throughout my 20s, my hobby was getting loaded. It was my lifestyle. I went to work – most of the time – and being a perfectionist whose self-worth depended on achievement, excelled at what I did, but what I lived for was "partying."

Actually, I always thought the term "partying" was stupid – when people talked about partying. For them, maybe that's what it was – getting together with friends, getting a little loaded, having a few laughs. A party. For me, it was getting wasted. That was the most important part. That was the whole point, wasn't it?

With my addictive personality, I took everything to the extreme, and by the time I was 30 years old, I had a full-blown alcohol problem. I wasn't much into any other substances by that point, but I was drinking the equivalent of probably a case of beer a day. I drank morning, noon, and night.

Eventually, my life crashed and burned, and I wound up starting all over again, pretty much from scratch. My first wife tossed me out after she took up with a friend of ours, and I wound up staying for a while with a friend of my brother's. A few months later, I was living in a tiny, one-bedroom apartment with no furniture – I slept in the living room on a pair of sleeping bags – and everything I owned fit inside my red Chevy Cavalier two-door.

Thanks to a well-known 12-step program that I was basically forced into by the court system, and some wonderful people I met there, I got myself straightened out a few months later. Sobered up, quit drinking for 22 years and had a mostly good little life.

Then, I decided to fully immerse myself in the local culture when I went to Spain the first time, and a big part of that culture is wine with meals, and so I started drinking again. I didn't overindulge at all – didn't get drunk, and didn't want to get drunk.

I told myself it was good to get that monkey off my back, so to speak. That alcohol no longer had any kind of power or control over me, and was nothing for me to be afraid of any longer.

For a while, that worked.

But as I slid slowly back into my depression, I started drinking for the wrong reasons – to numb myself, basically – and it started becoming a bad habit again.

———

CHAPTER
SIX

When Bubba and I connected on Facebook and started talking about pole vaulting, he was living in southern California.

He asked me which part of Texas I lived in, and told me he knew a guy named Brian Elmore who coached vaulting every Sunday at noon at a high school about an hour's drive from me. One thing led to another, and before too long I found myself headed down there.

When I got to the high school down on the north side of Austin, I drove all over the place looking for a track and a pole vault pit. The place was huge, and there were football fields, baseball diamonds, soccer fields, scoreboards, buildings here and buildings there, but no track.

Finally, I spotted another pickup headed my way in the massive and empty asphalt parking lot littered with countless annoying speed bumps, so I flagged down the driver and asked him if he knew where the pole vaulters meet, and he said, "Yes, that's where I'm headed right now."

Flashbacks to my arrival in Pamplona that evening back in June 2011, on my first trip to Spain, when I climbed the stairs from the underground bus station and had no earthly idea where I was, or which way to go to find my hotel. When I made my reservations on-line, the hotel was supposed to be a half-mile or something from the bus station, so I figured finding it would be easy.

No so much.

As I stood there on the sidewalk looking around, a friendly-looking señorita happened by and I asked her if she knew of my hotel. Luckily, I took Spanish in high school and earned a Spanish minor in college, so I can communicate in the language with varying degrees of success.

This young lady smiled and said (in Spanish), "Yes. In fact, I'm headed that way right now. Would you like to walk with me?"

So, sort of the same way I followed that girl to my hotel on the Plaza del Castillo, I made a quick U-turn, followed the guy at the high school down and around the corner of what appeared to be a small construction site, and we parked outside a big chain-link fence. Then, it was around the corner and about a hundred-yard walk to the far side of the track, where Brian and a few other people sat in plastic chairs, watching high school kids take turns running and jumping.

The guy I had followed – his daughter was one of the jumpers – introduced me to Brian, and I shook his hand and sat down, as he carefully watched each vault and offered tips and pointers, asking the kids how it felt, what did they think happened when something went wrong, move your grip up two fingers, go up a pole.

I was in no hurry to get out there and make a complete fool of myself in front of this group of a dozen boys and girls, which included a district champion, a state champion, and a national record holder. I wasn't even sure I could actually go through with it at all. I wanted to, but I had no idea what was going to happen when I got up there with a pole in my hand – and public humiliation is never high on my list of priorities.

So I sat for a while, next to Brian, chatted some, listened, and just watched.

Finally, after about two hours of near non-stop running and jumping, the kids gradually started packing up and heading home, until the only people left were Brian, one of his former students at the University of Texas who won a Big 12 championship in women's pole vaulting, an eighth-grade boy who was already getting close to clearing 12 feet, the boy's mother, and me.

Brian grabbed a suitable pole and showed me how to grip it, with my left hand as high as I could reach above my head, and the right hand about a foot-and-a-half above that (measuring the distance from my elbow to the fingertips). Then he showed me the mark on the runway to take off from, told me to take three steps, plant the end of the pole in the box, and jump, leading with the right knee, arms straight, trying to push the pole forward.

Uh, okay, no problem.

So there I stood. About 20 feet in front of this vaulting pit, one end of the pole resting across my shoulder and the other end on the ground in front, looking at that damn landing box where I'm about to try and take three quick steps, plant the end of this long pole, hang on tight, and propel myself safely across no-man's-land (where an awkward crash landing could not only be embarrassing, but probably painful), and feet-first onto the mat.

What if I look like an idiot?

Then, I thought about that old Journalism 101 lesson from the University of Houston. And I told myself, "OK, do you want to do this or not?"

The answer was, yes, so I gripped the pole the way Brian had showed me, took a deep breath and let it out, three quick steps, planted the end of the pole in the box, jumped, and – splat.

It was pretty ugly. I kind of twisted around and landed half-in, half-out of the box, barely up and onto the front edge of the mat. Not an impressive start, but I did it, and it was OK. I survived, didn't hurt myself, and nobody laughed.

Brian gave me some more instructions, told me what I did wrong, and I tried it again.

Second attempt was a little better, but not much. Same with the third. I got airborne both times and landed on the mat – which in itself was apparently a good thing – but I was doing all kinds of things wrong: trying to pull on the pole, instead of pushing the pole and riding it onto the mat; letting go of the pole and extending my arms out to my sides, which apparently is a great way to dislocate a shoulder.

"Don't let go," Brian said.

"The pole is your friend," his former UT jumper, sitting next to him, said.

My next three tries were each a little better than before, but on the fifth "jump," I felt a little pull in the groin muscle of my take-off (left) leg, and I had stubbed my big toe on the box that first run, so after attempt no. 6 went fairly well, I decided that was enough for one day.

I later found out that both Brian and Bubba were impressed that I had enough good sense to stop and not take a chance on overdoing it. As I was soon to learn, one of the primary concerns among older jumpers is preventing injury.

"Smart to stop," Bubba wrote on Facebook. "Most of us would not have. Already way ahead."

Brian added: "It appears John is quite a bit smarter than most Masters vaulters! He soaked in some vaulting from the sideline, got a grasp of what was going on, and then learned how to take off. Then was able to leave for home with no discernible injuries, or even a limp! Successful first step on his vaulting journey."

An hour's drive and two hours of waiting for six little jumps – but it was really cool.

I told Brian I'd be back.

———

Two weeks later, it was time to "jump" again. Part of me did not want to do it. That little voice inside my head that tries to hold me back, keep me down – put me down – and sometimes even lead me along a path of self-destruction, said the whole thing was ridiculous.

Pole vaulting? What the hell is wrong with you?

You are about to turn 60 years old; you're way out of shape; 30-40 pounds overweight; couldn't run a mile if your life depended on it; sore as hell from lifting weights at the gym last week for the first time in months; and you're going to drive an hour back down to Round Rock, spend the better part of a Sunday afternoon sitting and watching young kids fly through the air with the greatest of ease, and at some point, you'll finally get in there and probably make six or eight feeble attempts to perform a halfway decent take-off and flop onto the landing mat.

You really think that one of these days, you're going to sprint down that runway, plant the pole, spring into the air, swing up and through, and catapult yourself over a horizontal bar perched in your path?

But I did it. I drove back down, sat and watched for a long time, wanting to get out there and jump and not wanting to, all at the same time.

Not sure if it was providence, divine intervention, or what, but that particular day, three little junior high girls also showed up, wanting to learn to pole vault. It was obvious none of them had ever done it before, and watching them struggle with it the same way I had was somehow encouraging. Finally, after all the experienced vaulters had finished their workouts and headed home, Brian figured the audience was small enough for me to want to get out there again, and he was right.

My first little run was a vast improvement from the time before, and I actually felt like I was almost doing a decent take-off. I went about 10 more times, and was about to go again, when something told me that was enough.

Brian loaned me a pole that day, and I took it home so I could practice little three-step runs and jumps in the backyard. Getting that initial part of the sequence right was step one for everything else that follows. Besides, Bubba told me, knowing that the landing zone is hard ground instead of a soft mat, is great incentive for learning proper technique!

It was a couple days later that I took the pole out of my garage and into the backyard, opened up a double-gate in the chain link on one side to give myself a little more running room, and practiced some take-offs. There were a few clumsy ones, and then came the first major collision between old man and hard ground.

I figured out that I wasn't accelerating enough to keep the pole moving forward after I jumped, and this one time I went sort of sideways a little bit, lost my balance when I touched down, and bam! Down I went – hard.

It was a pretty rough landing, and didn't feel very good, but luckily I came through it appearing to be mostly unscathed.

After that, I knew I had to commit. Trying to be careful was not going to work. Apparently, overcoming the fear factor is a fairly significant part of pole vaulting, and like a lot of other things, hesitation can get you hurt.

So, I got set up again, rehearsed a little bit in my mind, tried to visualize what I was doing, and took off – three quick, hard steps and JUMP!

To my surprise, I actually did it this time. Right knee up, right arm fairly straight, left leg straight, hold onto the pole, touch down on the left foot. Ha!

Cool. I can do this.

A few more tries – some better than others – and I decided to call it a day.

Over the next day or so, my right elbow got more and more sore, until I could neither bend it nor straighten it out all the way. Any movement in that joint was excruciating. The arm just kind of hung there, and the only thing I could do was move it around using my shoulder muscles. Either that, or grab it with my left hand and move the arm where it needed to be.

Uh-oh.

———

CHAPTER
SEVEN

It took a few of those backyard practice sessions, but finally I started making some progress.

The elbow strain was coming from doing the exact opposite thing you're supposed to do when you plant the pole and take off, which is pulling on the pole.

Before I got into all this, I always thought pole vaulters ran down the runway, stuck the end of the pole in the ground, and pulled down on it. The pole bent and then straightened out, flinging them up in the air.

In fact, it's just the opposite.

When you stick the end of the pole in the ground (into the metal box at the front of the pit), you extend your arms as high as you can, jump, and push – not pull – the pole, driving it forward. If you're fast enough, and holding high enough, your momentum will cause your body to start swinging forward and the pole will bend, but not because you're trying to make it bend. That just comes from speed and gravity and momentum – physics.

Anyway, I had to lay off practicing for a while, to give my elbow a chance to settle down, and when I got back to working on the backyard drills, it finally occurred to me that I needed to get the pole moving as I approached the point where I jumped and planted the tip on the ground, close as possible to the outside of my left (takeoff) foot, which is sort of supposed to happen at about the same time.

Once I figured this out – finally – things started going a lot smoother. I actually felt like I was doing the movement correctly, and that was very encouraging.

The last half of the summer, I even managed to lay off the alcohol long enough to get back in the gym fairly regularly; do my jumping in the backyard; take a lesson from Bubba's coach, Kris Allison of New Braunfels, Texas; and start making a little progress.

Then the middle of August rolled around, time for school to start again, and it was back to work.

My training momentum came to an abrupt stop.

Any progress I had made soon faded, and I was back into an old, familiar routine – stopping at the first convenience store on the way home, catching a buzz in front of the television set, eating a little dinner, and going to bed.

In no time, this was an everyday occurrence that went on for about 10 more weeks.

Then, around the end of October, Bubba and his now ex-wife made their annual trek from southern California to spend a few months in central Texas, and three or four days after they arrived, my wife, Katie, and I met them for Saturday lunch at the historic Monument Café in Georgetown.

As usual, I was apprehensive about the whole thing, worrying that conversation would be awkward, that I wouldn't have anything intelligent to say – the usual yadda, yadda, yadda …

Of course, things went great. We sat in a booth, ate chicken fried steak, chicken fried chicken, mashed potatoes and gravy, chocolate Texas sheet cake, washed it all down with iced tea, and talked non-stop for two hours. Well, if you know Bubba, you know who did most of the talking.

But it was a wonderful time. A great visit. And not only that, we made plans to start jumping together on Sundays.

And the camaraderie and affection of that meeting with two people I'd never sat face-to-face with in my life somehow set me back on track – at least, partway.

I wanted to stop on the drive home from that lunch and get some beer, which is exactly what I normally would have done, but this time I didn't.

The next day, I opened my laptop for the first time in a long time, and wrote a little bit. I looked forward to starting my workouts again on Monday, getting together with Bubba on the weekends for vaulting practice, and maybe my first official competition on Dec. 30, two months away.

———

I met Bubba that next Sunday in a restaurant parking lot alongside U.S. 183 in Austin, hopped in his new Genesis sedan and headed down to New Braunfels, to Kris Allison's beautiful indoor gym equipped with everything you could ever think of for pole vaulting practice.

A hop, skip and a jump down Interstate 35 and we were there. I'd actually been to the place once before, when I took that lesson from Kris back in July. He put me through a pretty intense hour-and-a-half workout, and I emerged feeling pretty good about the whole thing – overloaded a bit with information, but undamaged physically.

That was not to be the case today.

Bubba and I warmed up a little – me probably not enough – and he started showing me different walking and jogging plant drills designed for a newcomer to learn and master the sequence of movements it takes to run and launch oneself into the air successfully. As I worked on those things, Bubba – who was nursing a slight hamstring "ding" – was testing various poles, taking short runs and jumps into the pit.

After a while, he moved me onto the runway and I started some little two-step jumps, learning how to hold the pole in the right position, let it drop into the box at the right time, and then spring off the left foot and ride the pole into the pit.

A simple move, but a little intimidating after such a long layoff. I got the hang of it again pretty quickly and Bubba moved me back, further away from the pit, and I started making longer approaches – four lefts, as he calls it:

Right foot, left foot, right foot, left foot, right foot – pole starts dropping – left foot, right foot, plant (tip of the pole hits the back of the box) and boom!

When I hit a fairly decent jump and landed in the back of the pit, he took a crossbar and placed it at the four-feet high mark. I was feeling pretty good at that point, took off – one, two, boom, boom! – and cleared the bar easily. My pole knocked it down after I landed, but it was my first cleared bar, which is a major milestone.

I thought jumping four feet would be no big deal. Kind of silly, really, and not very exciting when you consider the fact that I could probably get a good running start and jump over a four-foot bar without a pole, but it was really cool. I was stoked, and I went back to try it again.

This time, right near the end of my run, I heard a loud "pop" and felt a strong tug in my left calf. Uh-oh …

————————

That was the first in a series of injuries I suffered during the first year I was learning to vault and trying to get in shape at the same time.

Of course, it didn't help matters a whole lot that I was still drinking my fair share of beer during those first six, seven months. Because of that, I didn't make it to the gym a whole lot, and so pretty much the only thing I was doing, as far as any type of training, was going to New Braunfels on Sundays to practice vaulting.

Other than that, it was the same old routine.

Except for one thing.

I had started going to see that counselor that was recommended to me, every Monday after work.

At first, it seemed kind of like the same old, same old. When I sat down, the first thing she asked about was money – did I have the fee for the week. And she checked her phone a little too much for my liking, to make sure the 50-minute session ended precisely on time.

After a few visits with the "shrink," I had a follow-up appointment with the holistic doctor and she asked me how the counseling was going. I told her that I really wasn't feeling too encouraged about it, and she commiserated, but also suggested I give it at least six months. Give it a chance, she said, and then you can quit.

I said I would, and that's what I did.

And after a while, I began to connect with Lisa. She was open and honest, and she wasn't afraid to use some pretty colorful language here and there, as we talked. I liked that. It made her seem more down-to-earth. More real.

She also turned me on to a couple of really good books, including "The Mindful Way through Depression: Freeing Yourself from Chronic Unhappiness." This was the book from which I first learned about the concept of self-worth, and my lack of it.

I think it was this book, anyway. May have been another one she told me about. The important thing is that I learned for the first time ever why I had such low self-esteem. Why I depended on accomplishments and the opinion of others to measure my value – to determine whether I measured up.

When summer started to roll around, it was time for vacation, and time to end – I decided – what proved to be a highly successful seven months.

By that time, I had also somehow managed to put together 30-plus consecutive days of no alcohol, and was feeling a lot better.

———

CHAPTER
EIGHT

One thing I have never fully explored is the effect my mother's death had on my life.

We talked about it some during my counseling sessions, and I know it was life-changing, but even today, I still don't completely understand the impact it had on me. Looking back, though, I think it was probably monumental.

It had to have been.

I think my mother dying probably changed everything.

This was in June 2000, and I was still happily working as a newspaper reporter. Life was really good back then, and I loved going to work every day.

After a year of working in the main office, I was transferred to our one-man news bureau in a city about 20 miles away, where I was responsible for covering *everything* in that town and a couple of adjoining counties.

It was the best job I ever had.

There was a lot of responsibility, and that scared me a little bit at first, but I was pretty much my own boss, set my own hours, and worked my own schedule – as long as I got every-thing done, nobody looked over my shoulder.

One afternoon, I was sitting at my desk when the phone rang, and it was my dad calling. I think that may have been the one and only time he ever called me at work since I moved away from Houston, and so I pretty much knew when I heard his voice what he was going to tell me.

A year earlier, Mama had been diagnosed with a glioblastoma (pretty sure that's what it was called). This is a particularly deadly form of brain tumor, and she never had a chance.

After I hung up the phone, I stood up from my desk and walked around to get something off the nearby fax machine, and the room kind of spun around a little bit. My mind went blank, and for a few seconds, I just stood there, trying to get my bearings. I didn't know what to do.

I went back and sat down at my desk, called my sister, and told her I would be driving down to Houston the next day.

Her voice was ice cold and distant, as she snarled, "Don't bother, John. What for? I don't want you here."

Oh, no, I thought. This can't be happening. Not at a time like this.

My sister and I never had the greatest relationship in the world, but our mother's death would prove to fully and finally detonate not only the two of us, but the entire family. That's another story altogether.

As I talked about earlier, when I was growing up, I never felt loved by my father, and never felt like anything I did was good enough. I wanted so badly to make him proud – to hear him say those words – but it never happened.

Mama, on the other hand, was different. Honestly, I don't remember her ever telling me she loved me, either – I can't go back and remember those words coming out of her mouth – but she was a much more expressive person, fun-loving, a little more affectionate, and she said things from time to time that told me that she was proud of me.

For instance, she told me once about how she was sitting in the stands at one of my Little League baseball games, when I was pitching. I think it was my 12-year-old season, when I pitched two no-hitters and was the starting pitcher on the all-Star team. As I warmed up out on the mound, she said, one of the fathers from the other team, sitting behind her, said to someone else, "Well, if John's on today, we'll never touch him."

"I was so proud," she said, smiling that big, beautiful smile of hers.

It was one night about a year before she died when Mama called me at home to tell me about something that had happened at the doctor's office. She said she had been having some trouble with one of her legs not working right. She was kind of dragging the leg around a little, and it wasn't getting any better, so she went to try and find out what was wrong.

They did some tests, and found a "mass" on her brain, but it was the size of a pea and they were going to remove it, she told me. No big deal. She was going to be fine.

As it turned out, that was not the truth, the whole truth, and nothing but the truth, but Mama figured that would be what I'd want to hear about something like that, and she was right.

It was a shock and I felt a little numb – a mass in her brain? – but everything was going to be all right. Mama said so, and she always told the truth.

Even as I watched her decline over the next year or so, I never once admitted to myself that my mother was going to die. That was something I just could not deal with – I was in complete and total denial about the whole thing.

Consequently, I lost a golden opportunity – although it would have been extremely painful, and pain-avoidance has always been one of my life goals – to spend lots of time with my mother, preparing for the inevitable, communicating, talking about it, supporting her journey, getting to know her better, instead of pretending that it wasn't happening.

She even came to live with me for a short time during all this, and there were some really tough times – like when she called me at work one morning to say she'd fallen out of bed and broke her ankle; and the day she abruptly lifted her shirt up to her neck, to show me her withered body, crying hysterically and screaming about how unfair it was – and after a while, I couldn't handle it anymore.

So I took her back home, and left her in the care of my sister.

That's where she died, a few months later.

I'll always feel that I let my mother down in her most important time of need. She was always there for me, and when it really counted, I wasn't there for her.

Her memorial service was at a little country church in Iola, Texas, a small town near Bryan-College Station, where she lived for many years and was well on her way to a comfortable retirement after years of hard work as an occupational therapist, buying property and raising cattle.

When I walked into the chapel, it was mostly empty, except for my nephew sitting in a pew on the far side, head down, crying, with somebody consoling him. Mama had been cremated, so there was no casket. Instead, a small table sat front and center, filled with photographs.

As I stood there, the reality finally hit me, for the first time.

My mama is dead.

She's not here, and she's not going to be here. There's nothing left of her, but a bunch of framed pictures on a table covered with a white, lacy cloth.

She's gone, and she's not coming back.

It took my breath away.

During the service, my brother, sister, and I were invited to speak. My brother said something about acceptance, my sister talked about how her youngest son brought mama cookies, and I read from an essay I had written the night I got that phone call from her.

As I stood there at the podium, in front of a fairly large group of people, all staring at me, the first words on the sheet of paper I unfolded were my mother's name – Billie Jo Jones. I tried and tried, but the words would not come.

I was choking down tears, and I knew if I didn't hold them back, a flood would come and I'd be unable to control myself. I would not be able to talk. I might not be able to stand up.

It took what seemed like five minutes of swallowing and deep breaths before I was able to say her name, and start reading.

Even then, my voice was choked pretty much the whole time, but I did not cry.

The entire thing was surreal (that's the first time I've ever used that word). Mama wasn't there, but where was she?

Last time I saw her, she was lying in a hospital bed at her house, eyes closed, her right hand grasping onto the side railing, unresponsive for the most part, except when I leaned in close and whispered, "I love you, Mama."

When I said that, her face wrinkled up as if she were crying, so I guess she heard me. But she never opened her eyes or said anything.

A week later, I got the phone call saying she was gone. I called my sister to say I was coming down. She told me to stay away, and before I could get down there the next day, Mama had been cremated.

So I never got to say good-bye.

She was just gone. I used to say it was like she went away somewhere on vacation, but never came back.

———

I didn't recognize or understand it at the time, but my life started to change after that.

Mama was one person I could always count on. I always knew without question that she loved me, and was proud of me. I never considered the idea that someday she wouldn't be around anymore.

Hell, she was only 63 years old.

Looking back, of course, I took a whole lot for granted. Partly, it's human nature to take things for granted, I suppose – our loved ones, our good health, all kinds of things. But I've always been selfish and self-centered, and so for me, I'm sure that made it even worse.

The whole time she was sick, I was in such strong denial about the fact that she was obviously dying – even when she started getting her legal affairs in order, and made me her medical power of attorney – that I never allowed myself to face facts.

Instead of dealing with the emotions, going through the grieving process – whatever that is – I just bottled everything up, the way I always do. I didn't cry at her memorial service, and I never cried after that. I shut that stuff off so firmly that to this day I've forgotten how to turn it back on.

Nearly 20 years later, I'm still learning to allow my emotions to come to the surface. I cry once in a great while – shedding a few tears is a major release for me. Feels pretty good when it happens, actually.

After Mama died, the family blew completely apart, for a number of reasons. Vile, hateful, hurtful things were said and done, and some things just can't be unsaid or undone.

So not only did I lose my mother, I no longer have a brother or sister, either – which is something I miss. We never were really very close, but I can't help but think about what it might be like to have a loving relationship with a brother and a sister. I see other people who do, and it makes me wonder what I'm missing.

———————

Over the next year or so after my mother's death, I started getting restless. Unhappy with myself, and my life. Started getting bored with a career that I'd enjoyed for a dozen years.

By 2002, I quit my job working for the paper and became a public school teacher, which was something I'd never in my wildest dreams ever considered. I absolutely loved being a newspaper reporter, but for some reason, I wanted out. I wanted to do something different.

There was all kinds of publicity at that time about a shortage of school teachers throughout the state of Texas. I knew other people who were teachers, and I knew a couple of local journalists who had left the profession to go into education. Even though I'm a pretty solid introvert, and was never really fond of other people's kids, I knew being a teacher would pay more, and if there was this big shortage of teachers all over the place, that most likely meant job security. And I told myself that becoming a teacher would be a noble way to spend the next 20 years of my working life.

When I was dead and gone, I reasoned, being remembered as a teacher wouldn't be a bad thing at all.

However, I still wasn't convinced, so I started asking other people what they thought. Everyone I talked to about the idea gave me a positive response. The kicker came when I made an appointment with a woman named Ann Farris, who then was a deputy superintendent for a one of the school districts I covered for the paper. She and I had become acquainted professionally, and had a few personal conversations, as well, and I admired her, so I thought she'd be a good person to talk to about all this.

When I arrived at her office, we went into a conference room and sat next to each other at one end of a long meeting table. I told her why I was there, and asked her what she thought. Ann – Dr. Farris – said she thought my becoming a teacher was a great idea.

"Why do you say that," I asked.

She looked me dead in the eye, and said: "Because you're a good man."

I got a lump in my throat, and I told myself not to cry. Don't you dare start crying in front of her.

That was the turning point. If somebody like Ann Farris thought it was a good idea, then so be it.

Before long, I was enrolled in a teacher certification program at the local college, and started taking classes.

Not long after the big career move, I slowly started unraveling a little bit.

The job was OK, and I was doing pretty well. I was teaching 8th grade Reading in an excellent small-town school district in central Texas, and the people I worked with were wonderful and incredibly supportive.

It was something new and different, which was good, but teaching was just not a natural fit for me; not the way the newspaper business had been. Journalist was the best job I'd ever had, and although there were lots of good aspects to being a public school teacher – more money, lots of holidays, couple months off in the summer, regular work schedule that allowed me to spend more time with my youngest daughter – making the move was a decision I questioned quite a bit.

It may have been the very first day of school, in fact, when I walked down the hallway to the faculty restroom during a break, closed the door and leaned my head against the wall, asking myself, "What have you done?"

The job got a little better as time went on, but personally, on the inside, something was wrong – and getting worse.

Since I had never been taught anything about how to handle emotions, I had no clue what was going on. I couldn't begin to analyze or understand my feelings; I just knew I felt bad. That's the way it always was for me – I either felt bad, or I felt good, and I had absolutely no idea what was really going on inside my head.

As part of its employee benefits program, the school district offered a certain number of free counseling sessions per year through a local hospital. The idea was to help people having a hard time dealing with stress and other work-related issues.

I decided it couldn't hurt.

My first appointment, the first thing they did was sit me down in front of a computer for some sort of evaluation, answering a whole slew of questions about this and that, and the verdict came back that I was suffering mild depression and anxiety. Counseling sessions and medication were prescribed, and neither one did much of anything to help.

The counselor, for some reason, was fascinated by the relatively high I.Q. level I registered as part of the evaluation, and I wasn't seeing the point of our conversations, so I quit after a few sessions. It seemed like whatever anti-depressant they gave me worked at first, but that might have been due to some sort of placebo effect, because it didn't last long.

I wound up resigning from that district and taking a job at a school closer to home, which was good, but the decline of my, shall we say, mental health continued.

———————

By the time I hit my 50s, I was in full-fledged mid-life crisis mode.

I had written a couple books and gotten them published – which was really cool – but like always, the shine on that apple soon wore off, and I was in search of more satisfaction.

I wanted to do something "big." I had lived half a century already, and what had I done with my life?

Then, out of the blue, I stumbled onto something.

My favorite author has always been Ernest Hemingway, and one of my all-time favorite books is his, "The Sun Also Rises," which talks about riding trains through Europe, living in Paris and traveling to Spain for fishing trips and to attend the famed San Fermin (Running of the Bulls) festival in Pamplona. I'd read other things about people backpacking across Europe, just bumming around, and it all sounded so cool and exotic and romantic.

Too bad it was never going to happen.

Me? Travel to Europe? That was something that never came close to being on my radar, and as far as I knew, never would. That was something for people with money. People like me went to exotic places like South Padre Island for the big vacation. Going to San Antonio or Dallas for the weekend was a pretty big deal.

Like I said, I knew people from high school who had been overseas, and I was chatting online with one of them sometime around 2010, it must have been, and she mentioned something called the Camino de Santiago in Spain. I looked it up, and found out that this was an ancient 500-mile pilgrimage that stretched all the way across the northern part of the country.

People went there, put on backpacks, and actually walked from one side of Spain to the other. The more I read about it, the more intrigued I became. So I read more, and more, and more.

People talked about the spirituality of the place – remember, this was during a time when I was doing a lot of spiritual searching – and how the experience had changed their lives. How it didn't really cost a lot to go and backpack along this pilgrimage, walking all day and then staying in inexpensive hostels (albergues) at night, not having to spend a lot on food or anything else.

The more I learned about the Camino, the more I was drawn to it.

I decided that I had to go.

————

When I went to my last counseling session with Lisa, we both said – only half-jokingly – that I'd probably be back.

Especially after summer vacation was over and I went back to work.

But it never happened. Hasn't happened yet, anyway, and as of this writing, it's been more than a year since I've seen her.

And a lot has changed since then.

I continued to put together continuous days of being what I now call alcohol-free, and that has helped a lot. Looking back at the way I was carrying on, I really don't know how I was able to do what I was doing and function as well as I did.

Feeling better physically and mentally helped me get back into the gym and start working out again. I continued to go with Bubba every Sunday to practice vaulting ...

But, wait, let me back up just a little.

I ended the counseling sessions around the last part of May 2018, and it was just prior to that, in early April, that I entered my first pole vault competition.

A memorable experience, in more ways than one.

This was the 2018 Texas Senior Games, and I don't remember how I got talked into entering. I had a grand total of six months' practice under my belt (once a week), and I still wasn't working much at all on my overall conditioning, and so I wasn't exactly a prime physical specimen out there on the track that cool Sunday morning (or was that a Saturday?) in San Antonio.

There was a Masters woman there (in her 60s or 70s) who was the only female in her age group, and so all she needed to do to quality for the following year's National Senior Games was to clear a bar, any bar. It didn't matter how high or low the bar was set. As long as she posted a height, she took first place and was an automatic qualifier.

So they set the bar at four-feet or something, as low as it would go, and that's where the competition started. I honestly don't remember anymore, but I probably jumped at the same bar, since I had pretty much the same goal as that woman – just to clear a bar. For me to qualify for Nationals, I had to jump at least 8-feet, 1-inch, or place in the top 4 in my age group. I knew neither one of those things was going to happen, since there were six or seven men in my group who were not even going to come into the competition until the bar reached either 8 feet or 9 feet.

For me, a bar set at six feet looked awfully damn high.

When it was my turn, I lined up on the runway, nervous as hell, people sitting in lawn chairs all alongside the track by the pole vault pit, fellow competitors standing behind me, getting ready, completing final preparations, watching the competition get underway.

I was still pushing the pole then, sliding the end along the ground, rather than carrying it (holding the tip up in the air), and I think I probably started from "three lefts," meaning I was only six steps back from the take-off area, which for me at that time would have been 29 feet. I have no idea how high I was gripping the pole – one of Bubba's small poles that he was letting me use.

A few deep breaths and I took off running – I use that term loosely, as a 60-year-old fat and seriously out-of-shape guy does not really "run" – pushing the tip of the pole ahead of me on the runway.

Three … two … jump … splat!

Somehow, I managed to miss the aluminum box completely – the box in front of the pit where you jam the end of your pole and take off. It's a fairly big target, but my mind went kind of blank or something, and I forgot all about what I was doing. I think I may even have blacked out momentarily, since I remember kind of seeing stars.

Instead of sliding into the box, my pole hit the cushioned collar that goes around the box, or the side of the landing mat, and I careened awkwardly across the front left side of the pit. Luckily, I didn't hear any laughing behind me as I picked myself up and walked slowly back over to where Bubba was sitting.

He had kind of a smile on his face, said something encouraging, and I headed back up the runway for round two.

This time, I made the bar, which was good, and I took a few more successful jumps, wound up clearing 5-6 before my injured calf started bothering me again, and I nearly called it a day. The leg was hurting pretty good at that point, but I decided, what the hell, I'm entered and I'm here, why not go all the way.

So when the bar went up to 6-feet, I made three half-hearted attempts, but failed to clear and was satisfied to lay my pole down and have a seat.

After that, I continued practicing on Sundays in New Braunfels, drinking beer on the ride home from Austin, and the rest of the afternoon, as usual, and pretty much every other day of the week. Then, for some reason, near the end of the month, I decided to try and make it all the way through one day without catching a buzz.

I did that, and decided to go for two days, then three, four, five … and on day six, when I woke up early in the morning, I felt noticeably different. Clear-headed instead of all groggy, and in a fairly good mood, which is highly unusual for me first thing in the morning, even now.

I liked the way it felt.

It was either that day or the next day that I had a job interview in the morning – a co-worker had gotten a job at a different school and apparently loved it, and another position was open there – so I took off work, with plans to go to the interview, then go home and take it easy, enjoy the rest of the day.

I went to my appointment, which was around 8:30 a.m., and it lasted about a half-hour or so. Seemed like it went OK, and they said there were a couple other candidates coming in, so they'd let me know sometime later. Standard stuff.

Got back in my pickup and headed down the road, and for some reason, I stopped at the first convenience store, bought my favorite 40-ounce bottle of Miller on ice and proceeded to start getting shit-faced.

At 9 o'clock in the morning on a Friday.

The next day, I was pretty disgusted with myself, and I think at that point decided enough was enough.

Like the old saying goes, I think I was sick and tired of being sick and tired.

I remembered that feeling from Day Six just a couple of days before, and so I told myself that I needed to make it for six days again, to see if that same good feeling would come back.

Guess what?

That's exactly what happened.

And for some reason, this time it stuck. After six days, I just kept it going. Sometimes, it was just one day at a time.

For about a year, I'd been telling myself again and again that I needed to straighten up – especially since I started this pole vaulting thing. I told my wife there probably is no such thing as a drunken pole vaulter, and the topic came up quite a bit during my counseling sessions. But every time I'd set a goal, a day to start my "transformation," I'd cancel the date and re-schedule. I did that over and over and over.

By mid-afternoon, I'd say, "Screw it," and as soon as I could, I'd hit the first corner store down the road from work. Ice-cold 40-ounce Miller. Ahhhhh, so good.

And staying alcohol-free didn't get any easier for a while, even after I passed six days the second time, then 12 days, then 24, then 30 days, and so on. Around mid-afternoon, my crazy brain would start talking, telling me there was cold Miller waiting for me, and it was going to taste really, really good.

Sometimes, I could actually taste the stuff.

But I made myself pass by the store, head straight home, or straight to the gym. I started liking the way I was feeling more than I wanted to get loaded.

I was in love with pole vaulting, being active again, doing something challenging, and I didn't want to let Bubba down. I didn't want to let myself down. I wanted very much to do this thing. It felt so damn good to be running and jumping, being athletic again.

It's something I was born to do; something that's inside me.

The athletic bug and the creativity bug – writing, painting, music – are things that feed my soul.

Makes me feel alive.

When I walked the Camino that first time – after I overcame the terror and breath-taking anxiety of being 5,000 miles and an ocean away from home, all by myself – I felt completely free, and alive. Walking with a backpack all day long through the countryside, every day of the week, sometimes sore and tired, sometimes in agonizing pain, but pushing through it and continuing until the day was done.

Reaching the goal.

Accomplishing the mission.

It always felt so good; so satisfying.

Every single day, there was that wonderful feeling of satisfaction and accomplishment – not to mention the incredible love and affection, support and camaraderie from the friends I made there.

People like Tom, a Norwegian-born resident of Spain, and older version of myself, who even though we live on different continents, remains one of my dearest friends in the world.

Then there is Alf, another Norwegian who also happens to be a world-class Masters distance runner; and Paula, a born-too-late flower child from England who loves sunflowers; a South African lass named Nix, who only a few days after we met pulled a page right out of the Holy Bible when she used iodine, needle and thread to carefully doctor my sore, tired, blistered feet during a sunny afternoon somewhere on the Camino; and Jytte, a Danish healer who miraculously healed my sprained back by massaging and rubbing my feet and lower legs, and also tried her best to soothe my aching, homesick heart late one afternoon, outside a beautiful, centuries-old Spanish church.

Pole vaulting was giving me those same things – that incredibly satisfying sense of accomplishment and exhilaration every time I finished a practice session and learned something new. Making incredible new friends who supported and encouraged me; made me feel good about myself. Working through fear, frustration, fatigue, soreness, pain, injury.

Persevering.

Fighting through it.

Not giving up.

Not quitting, dammit.

I had quit so many things in my life.

My old man knew what he was doing when he tried his best to not let me quit football that year I was 14 years old. I was starting quarterback on an outstanding club team of 13- and 14-year-olds that every year played other club teams all across the city of Houston, and never lost a game – never.

Sometimes this team, the Owls, traveled to other states to play football, to other countries even, and never lost a game. Never even came close to losing a game.

This team was bad … ass.

When I was 13, I was back-up quarterback, and one day at school, the little brother of the starting quarterback told me that Greg was sick with the flu and probably wasn't going to be able to play in the game that night.

I was scared shitless.

The second-stringers, of course, had to practice against the starters every night, and those guys were beasts, man. Talk about intimidating.

I was actually going to have to play?

It turned out that Greg sucked it up and played most of the game.

One of the times I got sent in was to give him a breather on an extra-point try. Nobody kicked extra points in kids' football back then – I guess if there had been somebody who could actually place kick, that might have happened, but it never did. Everybody always ran the ball to try for extra points after a touchdown.

So the coach sends me in after a score, to run a routine play called "23," where I hand off to the number two back (tailback), who then blasts through the number three hole, between the center and right-side guard.

I took the snap from center, started to turn to my right, and about that time, the running back blew by me and into the end zone. I barely got turned enough for him to snatch the ball and plow into the line.

It happened so fast, I couldn't believe it.

The next year, I was the heir-apparent at QB, but not exactly brimming with confidence. Before I got to this team, I had become one of the bad-asses in the 8- to 12-year-old league, but this was a whole new level.

At practice one night, the coach – an old school, Bobby Knight-type of guy who yelled and screamed and cursed and threatened and humiliated his players – decided to single me out for one of his rants. I was the type of kid who only needed a pat on the back and a word of encouragement, and not a kick in the butt, to motivate me.

I'm still that way.

Tell me I'm doing good, and I'm on cloud nine.

Criticize me, and it cuts to the bone.

So this guy proceeds to dress me down in front of God and everybody, screaming, hollering, stomping back and forth, physically mocking the way I was handing off the ball to the running backs. Going on and on and on. Parents standing around watching practice are laughing, and I'm fucking devastated. Nothing even close to this had ever happened to me in my life.

After he is finished with his tirade, the coach strides past me and grumbles to one of his assistants, loud enough for me to hear, "I guess we're gonna need a new quarterback."

That was it.

Some kids would have reacted by getting pissed, and busting their ass to show this guy what they could do. Show him that he was wrong.

Me?

Just the opposite. I don't remember what happened after that, but no way in hell I was going back to practice the next night, or any other night.

My old man came home from work the next day and went to his bedroom to change before taking me to practice. I walked down the hall and told him I wasn't going.

Told him I was quitting.

"No, you're not," he said.

"Yes, I am."

It was a battle, but in the end, I quit.

And not only did that decision become one of my major regrets in life, it produced a whole cascade of other regrets, for a very important reason.

Something I'm sure my dad knew but didn't express to me, is that after you quit something the first time, it makes it a lot easier to quit a second time. And a third time; and a fourth time.

By that time the next year, I had quit all my beloved sports – football, baseball, basketball, and track.

Quit everything.

Now, with pole vaulting, I had another chance.

This time, I wasn't quitting.

CHAPTER
ELEVEN

After my first debacle – I mean, competition – at the Texas Senior Games, I decided I'd give another shot to qualifying for the following year's Nationals in Albuquerque by entering another state games in Arkansas or Oklahoma, New Mexico, or somewhere fairly close.

All the other Masters I practiced with in New Braunfels – Jane, Cyndy, Larry, Bubba – had qualified at the Texas games, and I wanted to join the fun.

What the hell? Maybe I could actually do it.

I went on-line and the Oklahoma Senior Games were scheduled for October – six months away.

Excellent.

That would give me a lot of time to practice and improve, and who knows what might happen.

So I registered, kept on lifting weights at the gym, going to vaulting practice every Sunday, working hard, following Bubba's direction.

Sometime during all this, Kris had an outdoor meet at his place on a Saturday, and all us old farts signed up. I was making quite a bit of progress and feeling pretty good about my jumping, so I was excited about it.

Lots of people showed up – Masters vaulters, young kids, older kids – and it was a beautiful day. I started warming up inside the gym where we usually practice, and after the regular starting-out stiffness loosened up, everything felt great, so I grabbed a pole and headed outside to start warming up on the runway.

Other people were already out there, lots of athletes and spectators lining up to watch, so I got in line and took a few little short jumps into the pit. Everything was going great, and then it happened.

I got a little ahead of myself, backed up to a longer approach and put a little more oomph! into my run than my body was apparently ready for, and … snap.

Just as I started to plant the pole and take off, a sharp twinge in my left calf stopped me in my tracks.

More than a twinge – it really hurt.

Oh, no.

You've got to be kidding me.

I stepped down off the runway, went and laid my pole down inside, and limped around a little bit. The calf was killing me. Come on, I can't be hurt again. I tried stretching some, jogging up and down a little bit, anything I could think of to produce a miracle.

This can't be happening.

Long story short, I had to sit out that meet, but I learned an important lesson.

After thinking about what had happened, I had to admit that I'd cut my regular warm-up way short. Usually, it took me the better part of a half-hour to get good and loosened up, go through my usual routine, before I stepped onto a runway and started actual jumping.

This time, I fell victim to my own carelessness – letting the excitement, anticipation, and adrenaline of a competition take me out of my routine. I probably only warmed up for 10 minutes before I got out there and started jumping. And when I got out there, I took a couple of short, easy jumps, then proceeded to back up to a longer run nearly right away and jump too hard, too soon.

Body wasn't warmed up, muscles weren't loose, and something broke down.

Simple.

When I explained my theory of what happened to Bubba, he said I was exactly right. It's not an uncommon occurrence, and something you always have to remember. He also said that since I had recently recovered from an injury to the same calf, this was probably not a major deal. What most likely happened, he said, was that "adhesions" that formed as a result of the healing process from before had broken loose, and although it was painful, would go away fairly quickly.

As usual, he was right.

It wasn't long at all before I was back in action.

One Sunday as we sat inside Kris' gym at practice, I asked Bubba if he'd consider going to the Oklahoma games to coach me, and he agreed, which was very cool.

I've learned a lot about the pole vault from a lot of great coaches and champion athletes, but I still have a hard time coaching myself. When there's not someone watching, who can tell me what went right or what went wrong with a jump, it's sort of a guessing game sometimes for me.

Of course, I probably know a lot more than I give myself credit for, but not only does it help to have someone who knows their stuff pointing things out – sometimes I really don't have a clue.

For instance, I went down to Austin one Saturday for a lesson from Ben Ploetz, a former decathlon champion in college. Decathlon is a ten-event competition that includes pole vault, and Ben is a really good coach.

I wanted to work on two things that day: my arm extension, and my trail leg swing, or kick. At first, I wasn't too sure I was going to get what I had hoped for out of the lesson, but Ben knew what he was doing.

After about 30 minutes of some really short little jumps, and tweaking this and that, I felt myself take-off from the runway, driving my right knee up, leaving my trail leg (left leg) down and back, pretty much the way you're supposed to, and then kick it at the right time to swing the hips up higher.

I was doing a fairly good job making that move at one time, but had kind of lost the feel for it.

And maybe the most exciting part was that in addition to re-gaining the feel of the kick, I also for the first time ever was able to rotate at the top and finish my jump facing toward the runway, instead of facing away from it.

There were several times during the hour that I'd make a jump, land in the pit, and say, "Nope. That wasn't very good," and Ben would smile and say, "Yes, it was – look at this."

Then, we'd watch a video on his fancy tablet that clearly showed me doing it correctly. More often than not, what I see on film surprises me, and looks a lot different than what I think is happening during a jump.

———————

The Oklahoma games were in Shawnee, at Oklahoma Baptist University. By the time they rolled around, Bubba had decided that since he was going to drive all the way up there, he might as well jump, too.

We drove up separately, and met at the hotel the afternoon before the pole vaulting competition. Bubba brought his six or eight poles, and I brought the one he'd been letting me use. Pole vault poles are expensive, man, and I didn't want to buy my own just yet, since I figured that as time went on, and I continued to lose weight and my abilities improved, I'd require bigger poles and have to buy new ones.

Using the correct pole is a bit of a science in pole vaulting. You don't just grab any pole and go jump. There are so many variables involved, and that's another thing I still need help with – smaller pole; bigger pole; move your grip up two fingers; move your grip up a hand; go to a bigger pole and move your grip down; bigger pole and the same grip; move your step back four inches; move your step up six inches.

About all I know is that if I jump and hit the bar on the way up with my feet, that means the pole moved to vertical too quickly, and I need to either raise my grip, or change to a slightly bigger pole.

If I stall out at the top of the jump and don't make it past the bar – landing on top of the bar, or brushing it on the way down – then the pole wasn't moving quickly enough. Either I'm on too big a pole, my grip was too high, or I need more speed/ energy at take-off.

It's too much of a guessing game for my comfort level.

When Bubba told me I needed to bring my pole – part of the overall learning experience, I figured – I went on-line and bought a pair of these nifty little racks that clip onto the side windows of the car. One on the front passenger-side window, and one on the back window. Lay the pole across, fasten the straps, add a pair of bungee cords for good measure, and there you go.

One thing about pole vault poles – they're very long, and not easy to manage sometimes. Again, part of the learning process.

At the hotel, we were on the fourth-floor, and the only way to get my 12-foot pole to the room was to carry it up the stairs. Apparently, sometimes hotels will let you leave your poles downstairs somewhere, but I didn't think to ask about that. For events like the National Pole Vault Summit in Reno, there's a whole transportation system in place for vaulters to get their poles from home to the arena.

But this was one pole, and not a big deal. Just carry it upstairs, and in the morning, carry it back down, strap it onto the side of the car, and head to the meet.

Well ... if somebody had recorded video of me in the stairwell trying to maneuver that pole, they might have been able to make some money on that funny videos TV show.

It seemed easy enough, but I was banging that thing into walls, getting stuck, stymied, and stifled. At one point, I didn't think I was going to be able to do it. I'd be stuck in a hotel stairwell with a pole vault pole. Finally, I figured out that if I opened the stairwell door to each floor, I could back one end of the pole into the hallway, guide the other end up over the railing, and make it up the next flight.

It was comical, I guess, but a little frustrating, and a lot ridiculous.

Coming back down the next morning, for some reason, was a lot easier.

Check-in for vaulting was 7 a.m., and we got to the stadium right on time. It was still dark outside, and it looked like no one else was there yet.

Eventually, registration got underway, and I started warming up – thoroughly this time. I had finally learned my lesson about the importance of warming up properly. There were a bunch of good Masters vaulters there – Bubba, a world champion; Don Isett, world record holder; Jeff Brower; J Barton Fogleman; a few others I'd never met before; and me.

I didn't feel nearly as out of place, though, as I had at the Texas games. By now, I had quite a bit more confidence, and I felt pretty good. I knew I had a decent chance at qualifying for Nationals.

The vaulting was inside, at the OBU practice facility, and aside from the competitors, there wasn't much of an audience, so I imagine that helped the butterflies factor quite a bit.

When the competition started, I was the first one up. In Masters vaulting, anyone in the line-up can request the bar be set at any opening height. Sometimes, the groupings are divided into two divisions: one for people who want to start with the bar at, let's say, 8 feet and under; and one for people who want to start with the bar at 8 feet and higher.

This time, I think, everyone was grouped together, no matter their age. Maybe not, but I don't remember there being a split.

Anyway, I asked for the bar to start at 5 feet, so I could make a nice, easy opening jump, and so I could be sure and post some kind of height. The worst thing – well, one of the worst thing, I guess – in pole vaulting is to "no-height."

So they set the bar at 5 feet, and I easily hopped over that. I was still pushing the pole at this point, and I ran from three lefts to start. I continued to be the only guy jumping as the bar went up a half-a-foot at a time, and I wasn't jumping very well.

I felt like I was getting over the bars, but it definitely wasn't pretty. Kind of just flopping over and landing less than gracefully on the mat.

In golf – which has a number of comparisons to pole vaulting, remember – it doesn't matter *how* you get the ball in the hole, just that you get it in the hole. Same thing in vaulting. Just get over the bar. That's what counts. No points awarded for style.

Good thing.

But even though my jumping wasn't real graceful or smooth, I kept clearing bars. When I made it to 7 feet, I think it was, other vaulters started to come in, too.

That was pretty cool.

I cleared 7 feet, then 7-6. More guys started jumping. The bar went up to 8-1, and by now, everyone was in the mix. I had nearly cleared 8-feet in practice one time, when Bubba and Cyndy moved the bar from 7-6 to 8 feet without telling me, and so I thought I might actually be able to make it.

Unfortunately, whatever I was doing right up until then stopped working, and I missed three times, but not only had I set a terrific new P.R. (personal record) of 7-6, I finished first in my age group, took home a gold medal, and qualified for the 2019 National Senior Games.

Amazing.

I was really happy.

———

It was back to work after that.

I rode that Oklahoma games high for a pretty good while. One Sunday soon after, at practice, Bubba told me that a friend of his who was opening a pole vault facility in Austin (Ben Ploetz) had invited us to jump as Masters representatives for his grand opening in November.

Wow, how cool.

Not only am I a gold medalist, but now I'm a damn local celebrity.

Who woulda ever thunk it?

A week or two before the big event, I tweaked my left groin muscles one Sunday, but it didn't seem too bad. Pretty sore, but I took it easy at practice, and there was no need to go all-out at the grand opening. Just get out there and have a little fun.

The big day came and I met Bubba down there, and before we started warming up, I noticed Bubba standing over in the middle of the main runway, apparently trying to get my attention about something.

Finally, I spotted something stretched out on the ground in front of him, and he had a big ol' smile on his face. It took a few seconds, but when it finally registered – what I was looking at – I was overwhelmed.

Stretched out on the ground in front of a smiling-like-a-Cheshire-cat Bubba Sparks was a custom-made pole vault bag with my name emblazoned across the middle in large red, white, and blue lettering.

My own pole vault bag.

It may sound silly, but I got tears in my eyes, and a lump in my throat. This wonderful guy was basically responsible for helping me turn my life around, and now he's giving me this extremely cool gift? I posed for photos with it, and then Bubba and I posed together, and I couldn't quit smiling.

Then, it was time to start warming up, as more and more people arrived for the opening ceremonies, which also included an Olympic vaulter from Cuba, now living and training in the U.S.

Once again, I was on unfamiliar turf, without the customary facilities and equipment I'm used to using in my warm-ups. So I did the best I could, and thought everything was OK. Then, on my first little jump into the pit, when I landed on my left foot, something tugged in my left groin area.

It tugged really hard.

I knew it wasn't good.

I don't think anything particularly unusual happened. I think I just landed a little off-balance on my foot, and pulled something loose as I caught myself. I tried walking it off, jogging up and down carefully, stretching some, and then another easy, little jump with a pole.

Major ouch.

No way.

It wasn't going to happen.

I told Bubba I didn't think I was going to be able to make it, and went back to the back of the gym by myself and tried to stretch it out, jog some more, but it was getting worse instead of better. So I sat in the bleachers and watched the grand opening from the sidelines. I had been nervous about participating, but now I was bummed.

By the time Katie and I got back to the hotel, I was in serious pain. Sitting on the couch, if I shifted my weight the wrong way trying to stand up or even adjust my position, it was excruciating. I screamed out loud in pain a couple times.

Crap.

Naturally, I took it easy the rest of the weekend, and then on Monday night, I think it was, I was sitting on the couch at home, watching TV in my boxers, when I noticed the entire inside half of my left thigh was a deep shade of blotchy purple, from the knee all the way up.

Good grief. I'd pulled muscles before, but never bad enough that there was internal bleeding.

I snapped a photo with my phone and sent it to Bubba.

His response?

"Cool."

I asked him if there were any one-legged pole vaulters out there. He said he didn't think so.

"Maybe I'll be setting some new records after all," I said.

Obviously, I'd done some fairly serious damage in there somewhere. Jumping was out of the question for a while, but I still worked out at the gym during the week and went to vaulting practice on Sundays, doing little drills and things that I could do.

Bubba had me start working out with a weighted sled harnessed to my chest – at first, walking up and down, then over time trying short tippy-toe type steps, up to jogging and then increasing the pace as much as possible without causing pain. I also wore ankle weights and a weighted vest for this drill, which is designed to strengthen those adductor (groin) muscles and prevent a reoccurrence of what I discovered is a nasty, painful injury that can happen over and over again.

It took a long time – that was the beginning of a 10-week recovery, and even longer before the pain was completely gone – but I haven't had any issues like that again, and I continue to run sleds several times a week, with ankle weights and a weighted vest. It has become part of my regular training routine.

———————

Next on the schedule was Jack Chapman's Expo Explosion pole vault extravaganza in Belton, Texas, just down the highway from where I live now.

I went to the Expo in December 2017, but only as a spectator. At that time, I'd only been learning to jump for a couple months, and had no desire to make a fool of myself in front of a large crowd of people. A year later, my participation was highly questionable not because of a lack of confidence, but because of an abundance of pain.

By the time the meet – second-largest pole vault showcase in the country – rolled around, I was feeling a lot better. I had bought some compression shorts, and one of these wrap-a-round groin support gizmos that velcroes around your waist and your upper thigh, holding everything together.

Bubba wasn't coming, so I was on my own, as far as coaching, which was fine. My expectations weren't real high, but I wanted to be there. All the gang from New Braunfels were going, and I hadn't done much jumping to speak of in a long time, so I was kind of jonesing to get out there again and at least give it a try.

I was one of the first to arrive that Saturday morning just before New Year's at the Bell County Expo Center, just off Interstate 35, halfway between Austin and Waco. Not real sure what to do, I took my two poles off the little window racks and slid them into my new pole bag, and carried that and my gear bag in through the front doors.

That apparently was the right spot, since the registration table was right there, so I signed in, got my goody bag, and headed into the arena. I had been there the year before to watch, so I sort of knew what to expect and what to do. I went around and down the steps onto the field, found the pit I thought I was assigned to, put my stuff down, then went back up into the stands to sit with Katie and wait until it was time to start warming up.

More people started to arrive, and about a half-hour before the competition was to get started, I headed on down, pulled on my knee brace, laced my shoes tight, and took a slow jog alongside the runway.

As soon as I started jogging, the injured groin – which had felt fine up to that point – tightened up. It didn't exactly hurt, but it was really tight and sore.

"You've gotta be kidding me," I thought. Maybe if I take it slow, and keep on working through my regular routine, it'll loosen up and everything will be fine.

Although it wasn't Kris' gym, and all the facilities I was accustomed to using were not there, I did my best to re-create my usual sequence. I did slow jogs, standing quad stretches, hamstring stretches, leg swings, walking pole drops, jogging pole drops, short take-off sprints to jump and slap a high bar, more leg swings, faster jogs up and down.

The tightness gradually eased up. I was hoping for the best.

Finally, I grabbed my small pole and got up on the runway.

Took off from 20 feet (two lefts), planted, jumped, and … it felt OK. No pain. Tried it again. No pain. The usual routine is three warm-up jumps from two lefts, so I went one more time, then backed it up to 30 feet for three jumps, and then 40 feet.

All appeared to be well – thank goodness.

After a really cool little opening ceremony, in which Jack personally presented commemorative 10th anniversary medallions to all the Masters vaulters, we got underway.

I was on the low-flyers pit, and I think I came in with the bar at 6-feet. I had plenty of height, but knocked the bar down with my pole. Same thing on my second jump.

Aw, c'mon, for heaven's sake.

Third time was the charm, but every time the bar went up to the next height, it was taking me three attempts to get over because my pole was falling back and knocking it off. Brian Elmore, who was officiating, finally came over after I missed twice at 6-10 and told me quietly that the reason my pole kept hitting the bar was because I was pushing it away with my left (lower) hand, instead of my right.

I got that little detail straightened out, and it was smooth sailing all the way up to 7-8, another new PR!

When I cleared 7-8, people came running over to me with big smiles on their faces, congratulating me for winning my pit. Everybody else had missed three times, and I was the only one to clear.

I won? I couldn't believe it.

How cool is that?

––––––––––

Two days later, on Monday, I noticed some tightness and pain right in the middle of my upper left leg (quadriceps).

Good grief – seriously?

My first-ever trip to the National Pole Vault Summit in Reno, the largest pole vault event of the year, was coming up the middle of January, and surely I'm not hurt again. Please tell me it ain't so …

As usual, I consulted my expert and Bubba told me it was most likely a case of simple "sunburn," a minor annoyance resulting from the extra exertion of the Expo meet after such a long layoff from regular jumping.

Chances are, it would be fine, he said, but I probably should take it easy for the next couple of weeks before Reno.

So that's what I did, and before I knew it, I was on a plane to Nevada.

———

CHAPTER
TWELVE

Kris had agreed to take care of transporting our poles to and from Reno, so all I had to do was get there.

Nevada is a state I'd never been to, and when I got off the plane at Reno-Tahoe International and the first thing I saw was a row of slot machines, I had to smile.

Yep, Reno all right.

Pretty cool.

Bubba was waiting for me at baggage claim, and we grabbed a taxi and headed straight over to the Nugget hotel, checked in, stashed our luggage, and headed back downstairs to the famed Rosie's Café for a late lunch.

All kinds of people were arriving throughout the afternoon, and Bubba knows everybody in the pole vault community – *everybody* – both in the United States and all over the world.

We had breakfast the next day at Rosie's with Simon Arkell, a record-setting, two-time Olympic vaulter from Australia. I met Sandi Morris, the top U.S. women's vaulter who won silver at the 2016 Summer Olympics, and rubbed elbows, so to speak, with too many other famous pole vaulters to even begin to mention.

The great Bob Seagren (1968 Olympic champion) was keynote speaker for Friday's welcome assembly, and wonder-boy Mondo Duplantis sat on stage beside a whole line-up of world-champion and record-setting athletes.

It was amazing to be in the same place, at the same time, with all these folks, and I felt more than a little like, "Um, what the heck am I doing here?"

We piddled around some during the day, went shopping for some new vaulting gear for Bubba, and rested up for the Masters competition, scheduled for 5 o'clock at the Reno-Sparks Livestock Events Center.

The day before, we had taken a shuttle bus from the hotel over to the arena, to check it out, and it was quite a sight, with as many as 15 pits and runways fanned out across the ground floor, and action taking place at every one of them. Young kids running and jumping, participating in various workshops and practice sessions.

Over behind the stands as you walk in the front door, dozens and dozens of long, multi-colored pole bags are lined up along the smooth cement floor.

More pole vaulters of all shapes and sizes together in one place than anywhere else.

Still, I felt pretty uncomfortable that first day, kind of following Bubba around as he continually ran into people he knew and introduced me. Everyone I met was really nice and friendly, but still …

Time finally came to get ready for the Masters competition, and then I finally starting feeling like I knew what I was doing. Bubba and I grabbed a shuttle bus over to the arena, and it wasn't long before it was time to warm up.

My quad was still complaining, but I figured if it was going to really come apart, I could at least get in a few jumps.

When it was time to get started, the official for our pit called everyone together – there were 13 competitors in my group – and asked which starting heights everyone wanted. I wasn't sure what to ask for, so I sneaked a peek at the paper on his clipboard and saw 5-1 checked by someone else's name, so I pointed at that.

It turned out that a woman named Carla and I were the only ones starting out at 5-1, so she went first and I followed. We both cleared easily, and the bar went up – to what I don't remember – but Carla and I cleared again, and the bar kept going up until other people started coming in.

At some point, Carla missed three times in a row and was out, so I moved up in the rotation and was the first one to jump at each new height. My leg was holding out just fine, not getting any worse or any better, and I was jumping pretty well.

In the past, it always took me two and sometimes three attempts to clear each bar, but this time, I was clearing on my first jump, and so I found myself standing off to the side of the runway for fairly long periods of time, waiting on other guys to make second and third attempts.

Pretty cool.

When the bar moved up to 7-6 – the same as my PR from a few weeks before in Belton – I was up and over again on my first attempt, and then it went to 7-9.

Oh, boy.

By this time, at least a couple of the other guys had gone out, failing to clear, and I was still in the mix. I was running from five lefts, gripping at probably about 10-6 on the biggest of my two poles, and I ran, planted and jumped – brushing the bar with my rear end but leaving it up.

I landed on my knees, kind of sideways on the mat, looked up at the bar, and raised my arms in triumph. The guy working the left-side standards asked me if that was a PR. I told him, yes it was, by an inch.

Now, all that stood between me and that elusive 8-foot bar was one more good jump. Just one more good one.

Unfortunately, it was not to be.

My first two attempts at the next height, 8-1, were pretty weak. I came up woefully short twice in a row, coming down on top of the bar on my second jump. The third and final attempt was actually a really good jump – too good, in fact, as the pole moved to vertical too quickly and I didn't get enough height before my feet kicked the bar on the way up.

Bubba said it was my best jump of the night.

Nevertheless, that was it, so I had to be content – and I definitely WAS content, not to mention thrilled – with a new P.R. at the biggest pole vault meet of the year.

Very cool.

I actually wound up in sixth place, out of 13 vaulters, and very nearly snuck into a tie for fourth. All in all, an overwhelming success.

We watched the rest of the action on our pit, and some of the other Masters jumping nearby, then it was time for the elite men and women vaulters to start flying. A sort of rumble rolled through the crowd when wunderkind Mondo Duplantis walked into the building.

I saw Mondo jump in person at the 2018 Texas Relays, and was looking forward to round two, but apparently this was not his night, as he cleared "only" 18-1 before missing three times at his next height.

We were planning to go to some fancy after-party at the hotel after the competition, but Bubba – who started getting sick and so changed his mind about jumping – had an early flight home the next day, and I was pretty tired, so we just called it a night and headed back to our rooms.

I had another day to spend before my flight home, so I saw Bubba off the next morning, then laid around a while, watching some football on TV, trying to learn a little bit about playing blackjack, before heading downstairs to the casino. The only time I'd ever really played blackjack before was on a weekend trip to Lake Charles, Louisiana, and I wanted to at least know a little bit about what I was doing.

Hell, I couldn't spend two-and-a-half days in Reno, and not do some gambling.

After I researched and memorized a few basic strategies, I headed on down, with a budget of $50 to lose – maximum. On the way to the ground-floor casino, I ran into Don Isett, and we chatted for a few minutes, then decided to have dinner at Rosie's after gambling a little bit.

Don took off somewhere, and I walked around scouting out the blackjack tables, finally mustering up the courage to sit down at a $5 table. I laid a twenty-dollar bill down, and the dealer gave me some chips.

There were several other people alongside me, and I quickly lost my first three hands, despite carefully following the damned strategy I had so carefully researched and memorized back in my room. The next hand, though, I won. OK, that's more like it.

Back and forth it went, winning some and losing some, until I'd blown through a whopping forty dollars. Don and I had talked about playing some slots, so I saved the rest of my allotted stash for that.

I went and found Don over by a bank of slot machines, and we sat for about 30 minutes playing five-card draw until I finally lost my ten dollars. Don wound up five dollars ahead or something, and we went on to Rosie's and had some fish and chips, then called it a night.

In the end, Reno was a great experience, and I'll definitely be going back. At first, I felt like a fish out of water, but by the time the weekend was over, that all changed.

It's like Bubba says ... if you're a surfer, it doesn't matter if you are brand new to surfing and can barely catch a wave, or the no. 1 surfer in the world, you are a surfer. Same thing with pole vaulting.

In my perfectionistic mind, if I'm not able to sprint powerfully down the runway, execute a flawless plant, swing into a beautiful inverted position, soar gracefully over an impossibly tall crossbar, turn and land smoothly in the pit, then I'm not really a vaulter.

Sort of a pretend vaulter or something.

When I was a little kid, everybody in the neighborhood got roller skates – those old metal skates with the key that tightened them around your feet – and skated for hours up and down the sidewalk.

Well, Johnny (as I was known then) got himself a pair of skates one day, but instead of heading happily out to the sidewalk to join the other kids, he went inside the garage with the door closed, where he skated around and around that little one-car space crammed with junk, over and over and over again, bouncing off the wall on one side and a large chest freezer on the other, until he decided he was a good enough skater to go out there and join the rest of the kids.

One of my classic stories.

After I got home from Reno, I sent Bubba a message and thanked him for going out of his way – which he did – to try and make sure I enjoyed my first trip to the Summit. This was his reply:

"After Oklahoma, I knew you were at a level that you would really appreciate it. And after a year of consistent jumping and battling injuries, you deserved it. It was important to me that you saw what others think of you.

"The biggest challenge I have for you is to learn to be able to see yourself in a more positive light. You do a lot of great things, and you provide hope and inspiration for others. They get moving, or show more belief in themselves, because they see what you have done. You need to believe in yourself more, and then behave in that role. Remind yourself that you are successful because you did the work to get unstuck.

"I know when I struggle with things, I know I've got a great friend in John Clark, and I need to behave as others would expect the person who inspires them should.

"Example: when I go to a meet or an event like Reno, where I know a lot of people, and even more know me, there is an expectation that I vault well and that I carry the same energy as I do on Facebook.

"Sometimes, like on this trip when I had a lot of work things to juggle, I'm not really in that place. What was cool was that seeing and interacting with those others lifted my spirits, and made me more effective at my business juggle.

"The lesson is that we always need to feel and believe how those inspired by us believe we should act. It's mind over matter.

"Everyone should be thrilled to have ANY fans. John Clark has fans because he is a great man. Honor them by being the person they believe you to be. Making yourself live up to that standard lifts you when other things don't work.

"Everyone knows your story, and I knew Reno would show you what they think of you. Congrats on some major life accomplishments and I'm beyond grateful to be your friend.

"You've made monumental changes in your life, but your brain and self-esteem haven't caught up. I see you as empowered, as do others. This whole exercise is to get you to see you more like others see you, so that you can enjoy all you have accomplished and motivate yourself more.

"Momentum is hard to get, but easy to extend. You're in the driver's seat. Enjoy the ride."

———

CHAPTER

THIRTEEN

That message pretty much blew me away.

I have fans?

People look up to me?

You gotta be kidding.

Me?

When I stopped and thought about it, I realized Bubba was right. They may not number in the millions, or the thousands, or even the hundreds, but because of my freelance writing, my books, and now, I guess, because of this physical and mental transformation I'm making at an age where it would be a heckuva lot easier to just sit back and do nothing, there are people out there who find inspiration in what I'm doing.

One Sunday morning at vaulting practice in New Braunfels, a friend and fellow Masters vaulter, Jorge, walked up to me with a big smile on his face and said, "Man, you're getting skinny – you look great!"

Later that same day, a guy who had brought his daughter in for a pole vault lesson from Kris – I didn't remember him, but apparently he remembered me from somewhere – said pretty much the same thing: "Man, you're an inspiration."

I certainly don't think of myself as an inspiration. With all the work I've done on my psyche, changing those long-standing thought processes, ideas, and attitudes about inferiority and not measuring up is a substantial challenge. It takes a lot of work. Constant repetition. An ongoing battle.

One thing I do every single morning now is, as soon as that alarm clock goes off, I reach up behind me, shut it off, and say out loud, "It's going to be a good day; it's going to be a good day." I say it over and over and over as I start my morning routine.

It doesn't always turn out to be a good day, but what that little mantra does is, it shuts down those negative voices that are always waiting patiently to start whispering in my ear. Those voices are powerful, and can be crippling. And if they get in there and get started, they tend to take over.

———————

Before I started that last round of weekly counseling sessions with Lisa, I never knew a whole lot about re-programming – re-training – your brain.

You mean to tell me that I can actually do something to change my thinking patterns from negative to positive? I can really, truly learn to like myself? Maybe even love myself?

That rare, ephemeral feeling of joy and happiness that I've woken up with a handful of times in my life can become permanent?

Or at least more frequent and longer lasting?

I had no idea something like that was even possible.

This old dog really can learn some new tricks?

In one of the books Lisa turned me onto, it talks about things like learning to replace negative thoughts that come into one's head with positive thoughts – immediately. When a negative thought pops up, and those pesky little things inevitably do, just say, "No, that's not true," and say (think) something positive.

For example, do you ever say things like this – "I'm such an idiot!" or "I'm so stupid."

Chances are, you're not really an idiot, and you're not really stupid. Tell that enough times to your subconscious mind, though, and chances are pretty good you'll start to believe it.

What is that adage?

"Watch your thoughts, they become words; watch your words, they become actions; watch your actions, they become habits; watch your habits, they become your character."

Learn to not say those things.

I've heard and read that people often talk about themselves in ways they would never talk about their friends. If they treated friends the way they treat themselves, they would have no friends.

A quote I found that is attributed to the late American writer David Foster Wallace says this:

"If you can, think of times in your life that you treated people with extraordinary decency and love, and pure uninterested concern, just because they were valuable as human beings ... the ability to do that with ourselves. To treat ourselves the way we would treat a really good, precious friend. Or a tiny child that we loved more than life itself. And I think it's probably possible to achieve that. I think part of the job we're here for is to learn how to do it."

Who knows – maybe that is why we're here.

One thing I do know is that I plan to spend the rest of my life – whatever time I have left – trying to become a happier, more joyful person, and passing on what I've learned to other people.

I've had people write me and say that one of my books changed their life, or affected them deeply somehow. Here's a portion of a review written by someone who read my book, "Depression Blues":

> *"From the very first chapter, I was in uncontrollable tears, thinking I was reading about my own 'depression-ridden' life. As I kept reading, the similarities did not waiver. Mr. Clark's battle, recovery, and honest self-reflection is leaps and bounds a better read than the typical 'textbook' types that make you feel more like a lab rat than a human being hopeful to find 'a way out'.*

> *"As I read through the last few chapters, I couldn't help but realize that my tears were gone - while a positive outlook on today took the place. Further too, I was inspired to continue on my (still in infancy) efforts to better myself of this dreadful disease. If you are even concerned you may suffer*

from Depression, want to understand what someone with depression is all about, or simply enjoy an honest man's story and care for others, I highly recommend you read this book!"

Amazing.

I was in a pretty dark place that August day when I woke up 60 years old, in a fog, another dreary day with little hope for the future. Now that I've stepped back into the light, I really want to stay there.

———

There were a lot of different factors involved in my coming back to life, so to speak, but a big part of the journey now has to do with physical fitness.

More than that, it has been rediscovering, and bringing back, an important part of myself that I let slip away for so long – athletics.

Pole vaulting has given me a second chance to discover who and what I truly am … and be that. Be myself. Really be myself.

Maybe for the first time in my life.

There have been other things involved, too, like that break-through therapy time with Lisa, and other self-discoveries I've made and things I've learned to let go of, but I think becoming an athlete again kicked things into high gear.

For you, that special something might not be athletics. Might not have anything to do with participating or competing in sports. You might not even like sports – it doesn't matter. What matters is what's important to you.

It could be anything inside you that makes you feel alive. An important part of your soul that you have been denying; holding back. Something that gives you a reason to get up in the morning. Makes you feel good about yourself. Brings you joy. Gives your life purpose and meaning.

What is it?

Whatever it is, I can tell you one thing that will make any-body feel better about themselves, and that something is regular exercise. Athlete or not – it doesn't matter.

When you feel better physically, you absolutely feel better mentally.

Something I learned when I was walking the Camino de Santiago pilgrimage the first time is that the human body enjoys walking – it is designed for walking. It wants to walk. Think about it. The human body truly is designed for movement. It certainly is not designed for sitting on the couch all the time. The body likes to move.

Get yours moving.

It – and you – will be happier.

Guaranteed.

For me, one thing led to another.

First, I got involved in pole vault. Then, I started getting back in shape. Along the way, I started feeling better about myself. Started feeling better about life. The ball kept rolling, and today, I'm still not walking around with a big smile on my face every day, full of joy and jubilation, praising the heavens for life itself – but I am most definitely a whole heckuva lot better off than I was before.

I'm optimistic and excited about the future, instead of pessimistic and depressed.

With encouragement from Bubba and others, I earned my personal trainer certification from the National Academy of Sports Medicine, with a specialization in senior fitness and nutrition. A local private gym I've been a member of for a long time agreed to let me start doing personal training there part-time, and I'm working now on building a clientele.

My hope is to continue building my Fossil Fit personal training business, and to inspire as many other people as possible who may have given up on themselves, and maybe given up on life, to get back in the game. Physical fitness and staying active is so important, especially as we get older.

It's more than important – it's crucial.

In order to maintain a good and satisfying quality of life, you have to be physically fit. Not as physically fit as a Masters athlete, necessarily, but at least strong and sturdy enough to be able to go about normal day-to-day activities.

———

The prospect of my death someday is still unsettling, but that's only natural. I haven't obsessed over it in a pretty good while. Maybe I'm just too busy these days. That final dirt nap is not something I think anyone really looks forward to, but in the meantime, there's a lot of life left to live, and I intend to live it to the fullest, and to the best of my ability.

Let's face it – getting older is inevitable.

No question about it.

As long as we stay on the grassy side of the turf and keep breathing air, time marches on. Nothing will ever change that.

However, there is plenty we older folks can do to continue living the lives we want to live, or have always wanted to live. Plenty we can do to continue the things we love to do, and maintain our quality of life and independence, even as the danger level of a fire, or at least setting off a smoke alarm, increases from the growing number of birthday candles on the cake.

I prefer German chocolate or carrot cake, please – a big piece. (Adding a scoop of protein powder to a glass of milk goes nicely with the cake, by the way, and that extra protein will also offset all those extra calories – wink, wink)

Along with a nice piece of cake once in a while, one of the keys to health and happiness – and longevity – in my humble opinion – is exercise.

Of course, exercise is beneficial for people of all ages, but maybe even more so for seniors. Along with the usual benefits of heart health, strong bones, and improved flexibility, regular exercise also is shown to decrease the risk of injury from accidental falls, reduce the occurrence of chronic disease, and even improve mood and help alleviate things like depression.

A major physical problem that accompanies the aging process is loss of lean muscle mass, also known as sarcopenia. After a person reaches age 35, muscle mass can decrease as much as 1 percent a year – every year.

Like so many things, the exact causes of sarcopenia are not completely understood, but things like lack of exercise, poor nutrition, and hormonal changes are known to be potential factors. The good news is that a healthy diet and regular exercise can reverse sarcopenia, increasing longevity and improving quality of life.

Weakening and inefficiency of the neuromuscular system affects things like posture, balance, and joint stability, making seniors more prone to falls, breathing problems, and psychological issues like depression. Lack of adequate exercise can result in such increasingly common health problems as obesity, heart disease, and diabetes.

Leading causes of death in the United States include not only heart disease and diabetes, but also cancer, stroke, and chronic lower respiratory disease – all of which may be prevented or reduced through improved lifestyle choices.

Better nutrition and regular exercise.

Not only that, experts recommend seniors engage in resistance training (weight training) that includes all major muscles groups at least twice a week, and up to five times per week. Strength training is not so much about building big, beautiful muscles – in seniors or anybody else for that matter – but about addressing the natural age-related decline in normal muscle mass and function.

Ongoing strength training helps older folks remain stable and sure-footed, preventing often devastating falls, and also helps them stay strong enough for simple, around-the-house, quality of life issues like being able to get up out of a chair or off the couch.

I have watched my once tall, strong, and active father decline physically to the point that he now is confined to a wheelchair.

It has been a painful, downward spiral marked by a series of bone-shattering falls, surgeries, lengthy hospital stays. I never want to go down that same path.

Generally speaking, muscle mass begins to decline beginning in the 40s, and increases significantly after around age 50. Older folks who lift weights two or three times a week can not only slow this part of the aging process, but even reverse it.

———————

The benefits of physical activity are myriad, including such things as:

Lowered blood pressure

Better immune system function

Decreased risk of cancer

Improved bone and joint health

Stronger neuro-cognitive (brain) function

Better respiratory and cardiovascular function

Improved gastrointestinal function

Lowered risk of chronic disease

Improvements in everyday functional abilities

Decreased risk of injury from accidental falls

Mood improvement

Doctors recommend seniors engage in 30 minutes of aerobic exercise a day – things like walking, stationary cycling, and/or swimming, for example. For those with limited endurance capabilities, that amount can be split into two or three separate sessions throughout the day.

Believe it or not, strength training is not something only for big, strong, young people. Seniors need it, too. Depending on one's fitness level, that can mean lifting weights, using resistance bands, or nautilus-type machines. Bodyweight exercises are also beneficial – things like push-ups, sit-ups, squats, lunges, leg raises.

Two to three strength training sessions per week is a common recommendation to maintain and even increase muscle strength and size. All muscles groups (chest, back, shoulders, arms, legs) should be worked by doing one or two sets of 10-12 repetitions. Movements should be slow and controlled, to prevent injury, especially to joints.

Stretching, flexibility, and balance exercises are extremely important for seniors. I'm in pretty good shape, a decent athlete, living an active lifestyle, and I have been known to lose my balance getting in and out of the shower, or standing up from the couch, maybe just turning too quickly, stepping wrong, or tripping over an electrical extension cord.

There have been times when I was glad there was a wall nearby to reach out and catch myself before I hit the floor or crashed into a piece of furniture.

Regular stretching helps improve flexibility, and it is something I don't do nearly enough. The days when I could squat all the way down to maybe pick something up off the floor, or whatever, are long gone. Now, I avoid going down into a full squat at all costs. Mostly likely, if I really need to get down that far, I'll just go ahead and take a knee.

Much easier.

Things like yoga and Pilates are wonderful stretching exercises, and also provide excellent strength training. I've done yoga before, and let me tell you, it can be quite a workout.

As I've said, before beginning a new exercise regimen – especially if you have existing health issues, and/or it's been a long time since you've been physically active – please discuss it with your doctor. If you don't have a doctor, find one. He or she will be thrilled to talk about improving your health.

———

CONCLUSION

Here is the part of the book where I wrap everything up in a neat little package, bestowing final profound words of wisdom that stir and inspire the collective masses to follow my lead, improve their lives through physical fitness – and even possibly achieve a long-given-up-on dream.

If only it were that simple.

I will forever owe a debt to the incredible sport of pole vaulting, and to Bubba Sparks, the tireless ambassador, world champion athlete, and all-star human being who I am blessed to call a true friend.

Pole vaulting has changed my life, utterly and completely.

And there's so much more involved than just the running and jumping.

Becoming a part of the pole vault community has been … uplifting, to say the least. Finding the perfect word or words to adequately describe the difference it has made in my life is really difficult. Think of looking at the most beautiful thing you've ever seen in your life – something so magnificent, it left you in awe; rendered you speechless.

Now, trying to describe that something using mere words doesn't really do it justice, does it?

Same thing with me and pole vaulting.

In what other sport would world champions, national champions, state champions, world record holders, Olympians, elite coaches – the best of the best – welcome a plodding newcomer with open arms? Encourage and invite them (me) to share the same practice facilities? Join them in the same practice sessions? Share the same equipment? Freely give training tips, advice, and congratulations?

Bubba always goes back to that surfing analogy. It doesn't matter, he says, if you're a world-class surfer riding giant waves around the world, or a weekend warrior trying to catch a decent set at the local beach – a surfer is a surfer.

Same thing with pole vaulters.

When I was in Reno the first time, I didn't feel like I belonged there at first, but my fellow competitors for the most part were warm and friendly, and I fit right in. We all cheered for each other, and congratulated each other on good jumps; encouraged each other on not-so-good jumps.

On the video of my 7-9 P.R., in the top left side of the frame, there is one of the men's elite vaulters (I don't know which one, but he had to have been at least an 18-foot jumper) jogging alongside the adjacent runway, getting warmed up for his competition, and he stops and applauds as I clear the bar, land in the pit, and raise my arms in triumph and relief. Pretty cool.

It's that way everywhere you go.

A vaulter is a vaulter.

For quite a while, I kept the whole vaulting thing as much of a secret as possible. To me, even though I was loving it, I was afraid other people would think it was kind of silly – an old, overweight, couch-potato guy is pole vaulting?

Pole vaulting?

Oh, uh-huh, OK.

Whatever.

I didn't tell anybody about it for a long time. Then, one Sunday morning at practice in New Braunfels, one of my training buddies, Jorge – who I had no idea was somewhere in his mid-70s – and I were talking about how much progress I was making, and how I was reluctant to tell people about my jumping, and Jorge tried to convince me I should be loud and proud.

"You're a vaulter, man," Jorge said, smiling. "Of course, you are. You're a Masters pole vaulter."

Since then, I've slowly been letting the cat out of the bag here and there, so to speak. A reporter from one of the local TV stations even came out to a Sunday practice and did some filming and interviews for a feature story.

The next week, I was front-page news in a local paper.

Falling in love with vaulting, and rediscovering my long-dormant athleticism, along with my growing friendship with Bubba, and learning some important things about myself and my psyche, produced a bit of a snowball effect. Now, I can't even imagine going back to living the way I was living.

If I ever do go back to living like that, it will mean that I've thrown in the towel. Given up – on life, and on myself.

The thing is, I've learned to think things through, and I understand now that my thoughts don't have to control my actions. I remember very well how unhappy I was when this journey started. I was exhausted, and had no hope for the future.

I didn't know what I was going to do with the final chapters of my life. I think I was scared, and felt like things were out of my control. I was sort of existing, sitting in the eye of a storm, trying not to think about the inevitable destruction that was bearing down on me.

Now, I'm back in charge of my life.

I'm taking action to make things happen.

To make my dreams come true.

It's never too late.

Sure, some of my life has passed me by, and I'd love to have that time back. But that ain't the way it works. Some of us are late-bloomers, and you know what?

Better late than never, man, better late than never.

Everything that has ever happened to me – all the stupid things I've done and all the time I've wasted – has led me here, to where I am now, and who I am now.

My life story is going to be a pretty good one, and it's going to have a great ending.

How about yours – what is your dream?

Since you've gotten this far, why not go to my website now, www.fossilfit.net, and take a look at some of the things I've put together to try and help other people put a spark back in their life and achieve a dream.

Part of my dream is helping you achieving your dream.

One way we can do it together is with *The Finally Fit Journal*, a special workbook I designed to help create a solid plan for reaching your goal, and finding and maintaining the motivation it takes to do the work to get there.

To get your copy of The Finally Fit Journal, go to www.johnhenryiii.com/my-books.

Purchasing the journal also buys you a FREE membership to my private Facebook group, where you'll find support and encouragement, answers to questions, and lots of great information from not just me, but an entire family of like-minded go-getters working to achieve their own dream(s).

Like I said, your dream doesn't have to be anything even remotely to do with athletics or physical fitness – although improving physical fitness is never a bad thing. Whatever that dream may be, we can work together to make it happen.

I've learned a lot during my journey.

Let me share some of what I've learned with you.

It's never too late.

———

A SMALL FAVOR TO ASK

Thank you for reading this important book. I hope you found it helpful, useful or meaningful in some way.

If you did, please take just a moment to write a brief review of the book on Amazon. Your reviews not only mean a great deal to the author, but they also help other people find this book. You never know, your review might touch someone's life, and make a difference for them.

Go ahead, take a minute now and write that review. It's important.

Go to the book listings page on Amazon. Scroll down to the reviews section.

Thank you in advance.

ABOUT THE AUTHOR

John Henry Clark lives with his wife and a formerly stray calico cat with a bothersome but slowly improving eating disorder in a one-stoplight central Texas town, roughly halfway between Austin and Waco. A graduate of the University of Houston, Clark is an award-winning journalist, author, athlete, certified personal trainer, freelance writer, photographer, musician, and artist who has written more than a dozen non-fiction books, including his best-seller, *Camino: Laughter and Tears Along Spain's 500-mile Camino de Santiago*, which chronicles two of his three backpacking treks along the historic pilgrimage across northern Spain. A tireless seeker, researcher and questioner, John has written a number of other fascinating books dealing with the human experience, from tragedies to triumphs and more, including his first published title, *Finding God: An Exploration of Spirituality in America's Heartland*, and the riveting, *Depression Blues*, in which he talks about how he learned to overcome a lifelong struggle with depression and anxiety.

FIND OUT MORE

To learn more about John Clark and his Fossil Fit
life improvement programs and services, including
The Finally Fit Journal, go to: www.fossilfit.net.

Sign up now and become part of John's team,
and start changing your life today!

Now matter your age or circumstance, it's
never too late to achieve your dreams.

Why not today.

www.fossilfit.net

www.fossilfit.net

QUOTES

"You are never too old to set another goal
or to dream a new dream."
—C.S. Lewis

"If you can dream it, you can do it."
—Walt Disney

"Aging does not necessarily mean letting go of your dreams just
because you think you are no longer able to reach them."
—Susie Harper

"Sometimes, people use age as a convenient excuse: 'I'm
too old to start something new,' or, 'I couldn't learn that
at my age.' Other people, though, go on to achieve their
greatest accomplishments in life in later years."
—Catherine Pulsifer

"But our 'childish' hopes and dreams for something more never really leave us. In fact, getting older can be an ironic catalyst for bringing some of those neglected longings out of the woodwork."
—Simeon Lindstrom

"Change your life today. Don't gamble on the future, act now, without delay."
—Simone de Beauvoir

"Where there is a will, there is a way. If there is a chance in a million that you can do something, anything, to keep what you want from ending, do it. Pry the door open or, if need be, wedge your foot in that door and keep it open."
—Pauline Kael

"Why not today?"
—Bobby Field

"Do not wait; the time will never be 'just right.' Start where you stand, and work with whatever tools you may have at your command, and better tools will be found as you go along."
—George Herbert

"You just can't beat the person who never gives up."
—Babe Ruth

"Be defiant and relentless."
—Bubba Sparks

"Don't watch the clock; do what it does. Keep going."
—Sam Levenson

"There will be obstacles. There will be doubters. There will be mistakes. But with hard work, there are no limits."
—Michael Phelps

"One way to keep momentum going is to have constantly greater goals."
—Michael Korda

"Why should you continue going after your dreams? Because seeing the look on the faces of the people who said you couldn't… will be priceless."
—Kevin Ngo

*"Never give up, for that is just the place
and time that the tide will turn."*
—Harriet Beecher Stowe

*"I have a motto on my bedroom wall: 'Obstacles are what
you see when you take your eye off the goal.' Giving up is not
my style. I just want to do something that's worthwhile."*
—Chris Burke

*"The only thing standing between you and your goal is the bullshit
story you keep telling yourself as to why you can't achieve it."*
—Jordan Belfort

"Only I can change my life. No one can do it for me."
—Carol Burnett

"A year from now, you may wish you had started today."
—Karen Lamb

"You're never too old, and it's never too late."
—John Clark

ACHIEVING DREAMS

Lots of people give up on their dreams.

Life happens; roads turn in unexpected directions; adulting kicks in.

Things change.

Honestly, looking back on my childhood, I was never raised to have big dreams. My parents never tried to squash my dreams – we just never talked about things like that. I loved sports as a kid, but I never dreamed of becoming a professional football player, or a major league baseball player, or a fireman, policeman, president of the United States.

I don't remember having any dreams like that.

The only thing I remember ever aspiring to be was, believe it or not, a dentist. I have no idea why, except for the fact that I went to the dentist a lot as a kid, and I guess I thought that would be something good to be someday.

Other than that, nothing.

I was a good student, and enjoyed learning, so I always figured I'd go to college after high school, but by the time I turned 17, my only goal in life was to get the hell out of my parents' house as soon as possible, and that is one goal I accomplished.

These days, I definitely have dreams and aspirations, but as far as written goals, that is something I'm still working on. A habit I'm still trying to form.

One of my dreams right now is clearing 10 feet in the pole vault. That's an achievable dream that is going to require a lot of work, which I'm willing to do. Another dream is to be "retired" and earning a living as my own boss through selling books, freelance writing, personal training, and health and wellness coaching.

All of those are definitely achievable – if I'm willing to put in the work, which I am. In fact, I've already started putting bricks in the wall to build that dream.

I've always heard that dreams without solid goals – a plan for how to achieve them – are just dreams. Most, maybe all, highly successful people are apparently good at goal-setting.

I did some research and here are a few things I found about how to achieve dreams and set goals:

Face your fears and take risks: this is a big one. Too many people, myself not only included but probably at the front of the line, live fear-based lives, and let fears influence our most important decisions. People led by fear are always asking, 'What if …?'

One of the things that had a profound impact on my life was that first trip to Spain, and walking the Camino de Santiago. I tried really hard to talk myself out of going on that journey, because I was afraid. I was terrified. Even after I got there, I wanted to turn around and come back home. By the time I broke through that fear – after four or five days of being there – I didn't want to leave.

Retiring from the traditional 9-5 working world, dropping that security blanket and striking out on my own is scary as hell, but I've been pushing through those fears and taking the necessary actions and steps to make that happen. Believing that it *will* happen. Fighting off those negative voices that tell me I can't do it.

Don't let fear determine your life.

At the end, win or lose, you want to be able to say, "I can't believe I did that," and not, "I wish I would have done that."

Take control of your destiny: You have the power to determine the quality of your life. Forget about the past (easier said than done, I know), and all the things that have gone wrong, either by your own hand or at the hands of others. What matters is now. You can either sit and complain about the way your life has turned out, or you can do something about it.

You can change your life *at any time* – it's never too late. Unfortunately, that sometimes takes a lot of work, and a lot of courage. You have that courage – everyone does. It's not some magical thing that some people are born with, and others are not.

Fear is natural. Everyone gets scared. A lot of people let it paralyze them. Prevent them from doing what they really want to do. Taking the easier road is, well, easier.

Courage is simple. To me, courage is being afraid of doing something, and doing it anyway. That's it.

I asked my good friend, Bobby, a highly successful business executive, about the concepts of fear of failure, and fear of success. Which one holds people back the most?

Neither one, he said. Not fear of success, and not fear of failure. Fear of effort is what holds most people back, he said.

In the end, I think he's right.

Make a plan: Dreaming is one thing; doing is another. Write down your dreams; goals. Then decide what it is going to take to achieve those dreams. What are the exact steps you're going to have to take to do whatever it is you want to do. Write those down.

Now, figure out a timeline that includes firm deadlines for when you're going to get each step done. Write it down. These deadlines can be flexible, but you need targets to keep you motivated and focused.

Break big goals down into smaller goals. Write everything down. Create a chart, a graph, some kind of diagram.

Take the first step.

Let others help: Tell friends and family about your dreams and plans, and ask them for help in achieving them. Not only can other people hold you accountable, help keep you motivated, and focused, sometimes they can provide resources and other assistance.

My friend, Bubba, has loaned and given me pole vaulting equipment. He has taken me places and introduced me to people who have provided me facilities to practice, and even given me instruction.

When we were discussing my becoming a personal trainer, it was Bubba who suggested the name, Fossil Fit, and found someone to design my logo.

Look at highly successful people, and remember this – they may be the big name, the recognizable one standing out in front, but there is usually a whole team of people standing behind them to make it all possible. Let others help. They are most always happy to do it.

A mentor can be the difference between doing what it takes to achieve your goals, making your dreams come true, and sitting around wishing things would change. Having someone behind you – especially someone who has been there; done that – motivating and guiding you toward the finish lane is invaluable.

If you're looking to make a change – and if you're reading these words, chances are good that you are looking for something – go right now to www.fossilfit.net and get in touch with me. Look at the services and programs I've put together with exactly that goal in mind – to help others make the most out of their lives.

Don't put it off until tomorrow or some other time. You don't need time to think about it anymore. Just go to the website and check out everything. Subscribe (for free) to my mailing list, and send me a message. Let me know what's going on. Tell me about your life; your hopes and dreams.

Let's get to know each other and get started.

I want to share my experience, strength and hope with anyone and everyone who wants to achieve their dreams.

It's never too late.

As my dear friend, Bobby says:

Why not today?

One of the things you'll find at www.fossilfit.net is a 90-day motivational journal I created that is designed to help you rediscover your dream(s) and take back your life, find new joy, happiness, and fulfillment. If you have trouble finding it there, try: www.johnhenryiii.com/my-books.

Look for the "Finally Fit journal" and get one today! It will change your life.

———

"The secret to living the life of your dreams is

to start living the life of your dreams today,

in every little way you possibly can."

—Mike Dooley

EIGHT-WEEK IN-HOME FITNESS PROGRAM

(available from Fossil Fit)

If you live in the central Texas area, where Fossil Fit is based, I have a number of in-home training programs available, including this great package:

Exercise sessions (half-hour) twice a week; personally coached by me

Education sessions (half-hour) once a week (nutrition, stretching and flexibility, etc.)

Two fitness assessments (one at the beginning and one at the end of the eight weeks)

Program fee: $929

Contact John for more information:
johnhenrytrainer@gmail.com

johnclarkbooks

MORE FROM
JOHN H. CLARK III

(Here's an excerpt from my second book, "Camino: Laughter and Tears along Spain's 500-mile Camino de Santiago." Although it took me a number of years after that first visit to finally get my life together, I believe this was an early starting point. This wonderful, magical place, and the unforgettable time I spent there, is something I still think about nearly every day.)

INTRODUCTION

It was probably the most frightening thing I've ever done.

Going to Spain.

I remember being basically held captive for hours in a bedroom at my in-law's house, nervously chain-smoking a box of Marlboros prior to getting married when I was 19 years old. Had a large semiautomatic pistol pointed in my face once when I stumbled into a pizza restaurant robbery. Watching my oldest daughter being born was exciting but scary as hell, especially when one of the nurses yelled at me for getting in the way. Riding a 1,500-pound rodeo bull was pretty scary, the first time. Getting up in front of a college class to give a speech is nerve-wracking. Woke up one time in a Harris County Jail cell in downtown Houston, and had no idea where I was. Standing in the front of an empty junior high school classroom my first year as a teacher, imagining a couple dozen teenagers staring back at me the first day of school was absolutely terrifying.

But the idea of traveling overseas, being 5,000 miles or so away from home, was possibly the scariest time of all.

For most people, I imagine, going to Europe is a tremendously exciting thing. Not a lot of people get that opportunity, at least not where I come from. I spent the first 31 years of my life in Houston, Texas, never living more than 20 miles away from the little 1,100-square-foot house where I grew up in the Langwood subdivision, near the Cypress Fairbanks area, across the railroad tracks and the old Hempstead Highway from Spring Branch.

When I was a kid, my family never went anywhere, and I never really imagined a world outside my hometown. Even after I graduated from college in 1987 and got a job offer with a newspaper 150 miles away in Temple, I didn't want to go – "Temple? Where in the hell is Temple?" – until one of my professors at the University of Houston convinced me it would be a good career move.

So the whole idea of going to Spain was extremely exciting, and also scared me half to death.

Even after I bought the plane ticket, I tried several times to talk myself out of going. On the way to the airport, I even had to give myself little pep talks. "C'mon, it's not like you're going to prison or something."

For one thing, I'd only been on an airplane two or three times, and never for more than three hours. Didn't particularly enjoy it, either. Three hours seemed like forever. I remember walking through the New Orleans airport after my first flight on my 25th birthday, deaf as a post from clogged-up ears. For another thing, I've always been a major homebody. I had driven cross-country a couple of times, gone to the Canadian side of Niagara Falls and a couple Mexican border towns, but to Europe? By myself? Any time I traveled any distance from home, by the time I got where I was going, I was ready to turn around and go back. I could literally get homesick going to Dallas for the weekend.

So even though I fantasized for a long time about going to Europe someday, actually doing it was never really a consideration. Little more than some kind of very far-off dream. Pure fantasy. Along with being a non-traveler, I never had the money for such a thing. Who did? Nobody I ever knew. Vacation was driving to South Padre Island for a couple of days, or maybe a trip to San Antonio.

Then, I reconnected one day via the Internet with an old friend from high school who has lived and traveled all over the world. Conversations with her, combined with a growing mid-life crisis, rekindled my European adventure fantasy, and eventually I discovered the Camino de Santiago pilgrimage in northern Spain. I did lots and lots of research, and found myself increasingly drawn to it. People talked about the spirituality of the place, the beauty, the self-discovery, the life-changing experiences.

So, off I went. And like always, it wasn't long after I got there that I wanted to turn around and come back home. I wanted to come back home in a big way. I even used the laptop computer in the hotel lobby in Pamplona shortly after I arrived to see how much it would cost me to buy a plane ticket and get the hell out of there. Fortunately, the price was outrageous. Unbeknownst to me, I probably could have just changed my initial reservation and come on back for a comparatively nominal fee, but I didn't know about such things at that time.

So I stayed. And I walked 500-plus miles across the country. And it was magical. Absolutely magical. The first three or four days were terrifying, but after I settled down and realized I wasn't going to die or something, it became one of the greatest months of my life.

I didn't take a telephone with me – which amazed some people – but I made use of various coin-operated computers all along the way for email communications back home, and also to chronicle everything in a blog. That blog (*entries in italics*) is the basis of this book, along with additional commentary I added later, so occasionally some information may be repeated. I met wonderful people along the way, from countries all over the world. We walked and talked and laughed and sang and suffered together. I've never felt more alive than during those days on the Camino. I hope you enjoy reading about it half as much as I enjoy telling about it.

———————

June 9

A rainy night in Pamplona, and I'm standing under an awning alongside the famed Plaza del Castillo, soaking wet and smoking a nice cigar. All the bars and cafes around the Plaza are busy, and people are huddled out of the rain, drinking and eating and talking and laughing.

I arrived here only a few hours ago, and I'm wanting to ask someone if there is a store nearby, where I can buy some bread and meat for a sandwich, to take back to my hotel room. It's been a very long day of travel from the U.S., and I am tired. I'm a little shy about my Spanish, so I wait for a friendly face to walk by. I spot a likely suspect and say, "Senor?" He takes one look at me, bedraggled and drenched, wearing a pair of khaki cargo shorts, a blue pullover fleece shirt and worn flip-flop sandals, and says, "No, no, no," and starts to quickly walk away. Just as quickly, I move toward him and say, "Buscando para una tienda (I'm looking for a store)." He stops and we talk for just a second and then he says, "You speak English?" Could it have been the accent? I say, yes, and he directs me across the plaza and down a couple narrow streets to a little convenience store type shop, where I find what I want: a package of Spanish ham, some cheese and a small loaf of crusty bread. Oh, and two ice-cold cans of San Miguel.

Like I said, it was a hellish day of travel that got even worse when I landed in Madrid. Finding oneself in a foreign country, without being fluent in the language, is not as easy a proposition as it might seem. Asking the right questions is easy enough for me – I took Spanish in high school and actually minored in Spanish in college – but the problem comes in understanding the rapid-fire responses. It took what seemed forever to find the right bus to get me headed from the airport toward Pamplona, and by the time I finally managed to get from Barajas to the bus station in downtown Madrid, I was seriously freaking out. As I sat for several hours waiting for my bus, I kept thinking, over and over, "What in the hell have you done? What were you thinking?"

I finally made it to Pamplona, though, without much real incident, other than a gut-wrenching fear of being stranded forever in a foreign country. Needless to say, my mind gets a little carried away sometimes. And when I popped up out of the underground bus station, a Spanish angel happened to cross my path and rescue the day.

She was the second person I asked about the hotel where I had a reservation, if they knew where it was and could they direct me. Both the hotel and the bus station were supposed to be very near the Plaza del Castillo, so I thought that I would have no trouble getting where I needed to be. As I stood there on the sidewalk looking around, however, I had no clue which direction to go. Someone later told me that when one travels to an unfamiliar place, it is a good idea to carry some sort of map. Oh, yeah, ahem, um ... good idea.

People were walking to and fro, so I approached a young man and asked if he knew of my hotel. He said, "No, no," and kept walking. When I asked the next person, a young lady, she smiled and said (in Spanish) that not only did she know the hotel, she was headed that way and would I like to walk with her? Boy, howdy, would I ever! She chatted incessantly and acted as a tour guide while we walked about 10 minutes to the hotel, which is indeed right off the Plaza. I didn't catch everything she said, but I understood quite a bit, and was mostly very grateful for her help. I must have looked pretty tired, because she even offered to carry my bag for me at one point. When we reached the front door of the hotel, she smiled and waved and walked away. I didn't catch her name, but I certainly said, "Muchas gracias."

———————

Traveling to Spain was sort of a dream come true. A fantasy come to life, really. I've lived all my life in Texas, and never been overseas. Hell, growing up in Houston, we never went anywhere, and I had no real concept of life outside my own hometown. As I got older, I'd often wondered what it would be like to drop myself in the middle of Europe somewhere, just me and a backpack, and travel around. Ride the trains and just wander from place to place. You hear about people doing stuff like that, and it always sounded really exotic and cool and exciting.

Despite the fact that I have never particularly enjoyed traveling, haven't really been that many places, and usually start getting homesick a few days after I go pretty much anywhere out of town, this urge and curiosity grew stronger over the years. One day, I was messing around on the computer and did a search for "backpacking trips in Europe." One of the things that came up was the Camino de Santiago, a 750-kilometer pilgrimage across northern Spain that began 1,200 years ago. It sounded interesting, so I searched some more. I read everything I could find about the Camino, which in English translates as The Way of St. James, and something about it struck me. Took hold of me, and would not let go. Although I'd only been outside the United States three times – a childhood trip with my parents to some Texas-Mexico border town; going to Monterrey, Mexico with my teenage football team; and a visit with my wife, sister-in-law and brother-in-law to the Canadian side of Niagara Falls – I decided this was something I very much wanted to do. Needed to do. Fly 5,000 miles to the other side of the world with nothing but a backpack, and walk by myself 400-plus miles across a foreign country. I had to do it.

I felt at that time like life was passing me by. I was 53 years old, and had never really done anything big. Never had big adventures. No major accomplishments, to speak of. Nothing really outstanding, at least not to me. Sure, I went to college and got my degree. Had a house and a wife and kids, a successful career in journalism, and was now working as a public school teacher. That sounds like a pretty successful life, by many definitions. But I knew better. I had wasted a lot of time in my younger days; wasted a lot of years. Squandered so many talents. Made so many mistakes and bad decisions. Blew so many opportunities. Fell short in so many ways.

People I grew up with and went to school with and played sports with had done so many amazing things. One kid who grew up a few blocks from me started his own company and became a millionaire. Another guy was star quarterback on his high school and college football teams, won a state championship, a national championship and is in his university's Hall of Fame. Another played big-time college basketball and became a successful major college coach. Others were doctors, lawyers, had lived in foreign countries and traveled the world. Hmm, traveled the world. Maybe I could at least do that.

So, I read and researched and read some more over the next few months, joined an Internet chat forum about the Camino, bought my plane tickets, started planning and buying equipment – hiking shoes, hiking socks, backpack, etc. – training on the weekends, doing more research. I was more and more nervous about it as the trip got closer and closer, but I thought I was pretty well prepared.

The big day finally came, two days after school closed for summer break, and I was nervous as hell. I told myself, hey, c'mon, it's not like you're going to prison or something. And off I went. The first two legs of my flights were fairly smooth. I flew to Dallas, found my way OK around that monstrosity of an airport, and then flew on to Newark, New Jersey, where I had a short layover before my connection to Madrid. The layover was something like two hours, so I wandered through the airport terminal to kill some time and find something to eat. When I headed back to my gate, I saw people lined up to board a flight. I showed a guy standing at the back of the line my boarding pass and asked him which flight this was, and he pointed at my pass and said, "This one." Good grief, I'd forgotten to reset my watch and nearly missed the damn flight.

On the plane, I learned that the woman seated next to me was heading home to Madrid, from a vacation with a travel group to New York City. She spoke no English at all, so I decided this was a good opportunity to try out some of my Spanish. We talked quite a bit – sometimes successfully; sometimes not so much – but it was fun, and I asked her to write something in my journal. She wrote (in Spanish, of course): "To a very nice gentleman, I hope you have a great time on the Camino de Santiago." Pretty cool.

It was a long, long overnight flight, and I was probably the only passenger who did not sleep at all. Not one bit. I tried, but it just wasn't happening. I had a little bag with me, containing all the essentials for a long flight that I'd read about – saline nasal spray, ear plugs, Tylenol PM – and I dutifully used all those things. But my restless leg syndrome and my anxiety kicked in, and so I stood beside my seat for a while, walked up and down the aisle for a while, stood at the back of the plane for a while, sat for a while, stood for a while, sat for a while.

Finally, we landed at Barajas and I went through customs and got my passport stamped, picked up my black duffel bag containing my backpack, hiking shoes and trekking pole, and headed outside the terminal. People on the Camino chat forum had told me exactly what to do to get to Pamplona, but I didn't write anything down. I don't know why I didn't write myself some reminders. I just didn't. Didn't even think about it. I guess I thought I knew what to do. It sounded easy, but as soon as I stepped outside, I promptly forgot everything I'd been told.

I thought I'd be able to take a bus straight from the airport to Pamplona, but I could not find one. Buses were everywhere and were bound for a wide array of cities, but none for Pamplona that I could find. I'm tired as hell, probably jet-lagged, kind of brain-dead, and dragging this increasingly heavy duffel bag around, back and forth, up and down, trying to figure out how to get where I need to be. I asked a few airport people standing around, but they weren't real helpful. Severe communication breakdown. I'm getting a little exasperated at this point, wondering if I'll ever find the right bus. Is there a right bus? What am I doing to do? Finally, I remember something about looking for a bus no. 200, and I spot one, way over there. I walk over and say something to the driver about going to Pamplona. The expression on my face must have given away my growing desperation, and the pretty young girl sitting behind the wheel smiled and said in English, "Take this bus, get off at the last stop and go upstairs."

Big smile. "Gracias." I was so relieved.

The bus took me to the downtown bus station, and I followed a crowd up a long set of stairs and found the ticket sales area. I waited in line for several minutes, stepped up to a window and was not-so-politely told that I needed to take a number. Normally, that probably would have pissed me off pretty good. But now, so tired and disoriented, I obediently turned and walked to the number-dispensing machine, pulled a ticket and got back in line. When it was my turn again, I said, "Pamplona," handed over about 25 euros, got my bus ticket and sat down to wait for the 3 o'clock bus.

As the time crawled by, my mind started to get the best of me again. I watched people walking around, talking on cell phones, and all I could think about was how very far away I was from home. Sitting in sort of a dingy bus station somewhere in downtown Madrid, knowing absolutely nobody. I had decided not to take a phone with me, and rely on calling cards if I needed to make a call, so I was truly all alone. Part of what I wrote in my journal while I sat there included, "I'm really pretty much freaking out." I was basically home-free at this point, but … would the bus be here on time? Would it be late? Would I get on the right bus? What if I miss the bus?

I kept thinking, "What have you done? What were you thinking? Why in the hell did you come here?" I tried not to think about how far I actually was from home. I walked outside several times to where the buses come in, to check and re-check the bay number for my bus. Stood out there for a while. Went back inside and sat on a bench. Rustled around in my duffel bag a little bit. Watched the clock. Bought a bottle of water from a vending machine. Listened to the garbled arrival and departure announcements that I could not fully understand. Finally, around 2:30 p.m., I walked outside and just stood there.

Sure enough, the bus was right on time. I watched as other people walked around and slid their bags into the big luggage compartment on the outside of the bus. So I queued up and heaved my duffel bag in there, showed the driver my ticket and climbed aboard. Now, I'm feeling a little better, but still a bit nervous about a transfer I have to make in some place called Soria. The bus is big and new and nice, and it's a pleasant, comfortable trip. Two seats ahead of me is a mother and her teenage son. She's a hottie and he's a good-looking kid, probably about 16 or 17, who has a cell phone plugged into a laptop computer and seems to be skypeing or something most of the trip. He turns the open laptop to face the window, holds it close to his face and carries on a whispered conversation with somebody. Pretty interesting.

Eventually, I arrive at the Pamplona bus station, meet my Spanish angel and check in at the hotel. When I turned the key (an actual key; not a magnetic card) and opened the door to my room, I was a little surprised at how small it was – roughly the size of a large walk-in closet, with a tiny bathroom and a small window looking out on a brick wall. Wow. I'd heard European hotel rooms were small, but ….

After exploring the Plaza, walking around in the rain and buying some sandwich-makings and two tall cans of San Miguel,

I returned to my miniature room, ate dinner while sitting on the bed and watching some Spanish TV news stations, then took a warm bath in the itty-bitty tub. The thing couldn't have been much more than two feet wide and four feet long. It was really small. But I really like baths, so I filled it up with hot water and wedged my six-feet, two-inches in there. It was comforting. Kind of pitiful, I guess, but comforting. After that, I took out my Camino guidebook and looked at a small map of the central part of the city, and made plans for the next day. I have decided to stay here an extra night, to recuperate from the travel day and rest up for the start of my Camino.

————

johnclarkbooks

For more on John and his books, along with information on his writing services, visit: www.johnhenryiii.com.

To find out more about his Fossil Fit senior fitness program, personal training, health and wellness coaching, and other products and services, go to: www.fossilfit.net.

Find John on Facebook at:
https://www.facebook.com/finallyfit
https://www.facebook.com/johnclarkbooks/

Made in the USA
Middletown, DE
04 August 2020